Prayers from the Heart

Publications International, Ltd.

Scripture quotations from *The Holy Bible, King James Version*

Images from Shutterstock.com

Louis Weber, CEO
Publications International, Ltd.
8140 Lehigh Avenue
Morton Grove, IL 60053

ISBN: 978-1-63938-809-7

Manufactured in China.

8 7 6 5 4 3 2 1

Let's get social!

@Publications_International

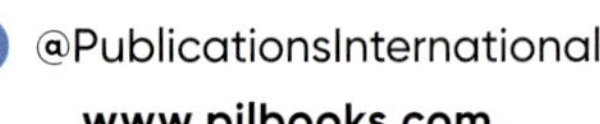
@PublicationsInternational

www.pilbooks.com

January 1

Lord, this year I pray I will stop taking all your miraculous works for granted. Whether I praise you through song, words, or actions, I want to praise you not only for what you are doing, but also for all you have done in the past. Help me see the holiness of the ordinary in each day of this New Year.

January 2

Thank you, Lord, for the hobbies that I enjoy. How much joy I get out of these pleasures! Thank you for the chance to create, play, and enjoy. I am grateful for the people who share my hobby and who have become my friends. What a gift to share the joy of our pastimes together!

January 3

Dear God, help us work to live instead of living just to work. Lead us to the green pastures where we can enjoy the companionship of our loved ones and the pleasures that restore us.

January 4

Almighty God, sometimes the floods of life leave us devastated and defeated. Our tears flow like rivers pushing over their banks. In those moments, please give us comfort and hope.

January 5

Only machines run perfectly—for awhile—and we know exactly what to expect from them. But we are different, Lord. We often do the unexpected, certainly the imperfect.

Give us the joy of diversity and the pleasure of indulging variety in our approaches to life. Being incomplete, we reach our hands to you, expecting help. And that is good, since only in you can we be perfectly fulfilled.

January 6

It is so easy to become overwhelmed, O faithful Spirit, by the needs surrounding us. Our voices join with the faithful through the centuries who have pleaded for the coming of your kingdom, for an end to the violence and suffering. We have prayed for restitution and justice to overcome deceit and despair. Give us strength to continue to do our part, courage to stand apart, and compassion to reach out to those who have been torn apart by their life experiences. Help us change the world with you, one moment at a time.

January 7

When trouble strikes, O God, we are restored by small signs of hope found in ordinary places: friends, random kindness, shared pain, and support. Help us collect them like mustard seeds that can grow into a spreading harvest of well-being.

January 8

God, a call, a note, and a handclasp from a friend are simple and seemingly insignificant. Yet you inspire these gifts from people we have a special affection for. These cherished acts of friendship nudge aside doubts about who we are when we feel low and encourage our hearts in a way that lifts our spirits. Thank you for the friends you have given us.

January 9

I ask you to cleanse my heart today of all lingering resentments. I say I forgive something, but sometimes I have a hard time letting it go—I want someone to see my side and tell me I was right! But I want to walk free into the New Year. Please help me let go of any bitterness or anger I am holding onto, so that I can keep my hands open to receive your mercy and grace.

January 10

God, you are so great. It is always the right time to worship you, but morning is best. Praise for the dawning light that streams in through this window. Praise for the sound of the birds as they flit through in the air. Praise for the little spider crawling along on the ceiling. Praise for the smell of coffee and the warmth of a cup in my hands. Praise for the flowering plants—and even those weeds growing by the house. Praise for the neighbors walking along the sidewalk and the clouds moving by, too. Most of all, praise for the breath that keeps flowing in and out of my lungs. Yes, this is the greatest item of praise: that you alone are my life—all life itself. Without you, all is dust.

January 11

Lord, you send sunlight and rain in equal measure. How can I be thankful for one and not the other? Help me see the beauty in both. I ask for your gifts of grace and peace and an extra dose of resourcefulness to help me survive.

January 12

Thank you Lord, for each new sunrise we witness. Sunrises remind us that we too can make a fresh start and try our best.

January 13

Today I am thankful for the gift of laughter. How wonderful it is to let out a big belly laugh and feel joy rush through my entire body! Thank you for the people who make me laugh, whether it is a neighbor or friend or a performer on television. Thank you for allowing me to experience joy bursting out of me, and help me make others feel happy with my laughter as well.

January 14

Lord, the familiar is disappearing from neighborhood and nature, and we grieve the loss. Yet, we're resurrection people, unafraid of endings because of the promise of beginnings. On the other hand, we must learn restraint: Help us, God, to temper our actions with wisdom.

January 15

We know you, Lord, in the changing seasons: in leaves blazing gently in fall beauty and in winter's snow sculptures. We know you in arid desert cactus blooms and in the migration of whales and the spawn of fish and turtles. In the blending of the seasons, we feel your renewing, steadfast care, and worries lose their power to overwhelm. The list of your hope-filled marvels is endless, and our gratitude is equally so.

January 16

God, it's a quiet winter day. Help me pause to listen to you, to talk to you, to enjoy your company. Chase away my guilt and shame and fear, and draw me close to your heart. Remind me that no matter what my earthly roles may be, in your presence I am your child, and you care for me more than I could ever imagine. Let me lean against your heart now, Father, and hear it beating with love for me.

January 17

Remind me of this, Lord: guidance is there, but I must look with my heart. I must let go of what the mind and ego see, for it is not the truth. I must follow where my heart leads, for it is led by the spirit of a loving and powerful God who wants what is best for me!

January 18

I may not understand your ways, God, or what your plans are for me, but I trust you. I know you have my best interests always at heart, and you won't lead me astray. My trust in your will acts like a lighthouse beacon guiding me safely to shore.

January 19

I am feeling tired and weary and weak. I do my best each day, and often it doesn't seem good enough. I lose hope and enthusiasm and a sense of purpose to carry on. I pray today for restored hope in my heart, and a new vision of possibility in my soul. I pray you will assure me of better days to come, and that in the meantime, I am never alone in my struggles. I pray for a rejuvenated body with energy to continue to pursue my passions and dreams. Give me hope again, God, because my life is not over yet. Take my hand and pull me up just enough that I can get on my feet again and keep moving forward.

January 20

God, the blessed feeling of being at home in your loving presence is like nothing else. The joy I feel when I know I never walk alone is the greatest of gifts, and when I look around at the wonderful people you have chosen to walk with me through life—my family and my friends—I truly know that I am loved. Thank you, God, for these miracles, and for these blessings, far too numerous to count. And to think I never have to look too far from home to find them is the best miracle of all.

January 21

God, give me the wisdom to know what is important in life, and the courage to pursue those things. My life is such a blur lately, with an overload of obligations, information, and distractions coming at me to the point where I end up feeling so very tired and worn down. I'm not getting things done, and failing to take care of my own health. Help me slow down and focus. Help me not be afraid to say no. Give me strength to tackle the important duties, which then leave room for more fun in my life. Show me, God, balance and harmony between what I need to do for others, and what I need to replenish myself.

January 22

God, give me the insight to discern your will for me. Help me to ignore those who may not have my best interests at heart. Give me strength to stay on my own path until I achieve my goals.

January 23

Give me the tools for building peace, O God, when tempers flare—inside and outside these four walls. May I use your wisdom and share it. May I remember that my tools include a kind heart and faith. Help me to remember that each tiny rebuilt bridge is a triumph.

January 24

I thank you for the healing power of friends and for the positive emotions friendship brings. Thank you for sending companions to me so we can support and encourage one another and share our joys and sorrows. My friends represent for me your presence and friendship here in this world. Please keep them in your care, Father. We need each other, and we need you.

January 25

Lord, let my light shine brightly, even if it makes me feel uncomfortable. I am not used to standing in the spotlight. But you have convinced me that there is nothing wrong with feeling the love of who I am in your eyes, so help me get over the feeling of embarrassment and let my talents and gifts reveal themselves. There is no pride in letting the lamp of love you have lit within me give forth its glorious light. Show me how to enlighten the world and yet stay humble and grateful and true.

January 26

When my own strength fails me, I turn to God. When my heart quivers in fear, I turn to God. When I am scared and don't know what to do next, I turn to God. There are times when my own strength is enough, but when it isn't, I know that if I fall, God is always present to pick me up and carry me. With God at my side, my fear vanishes and my courage returns.

January 27

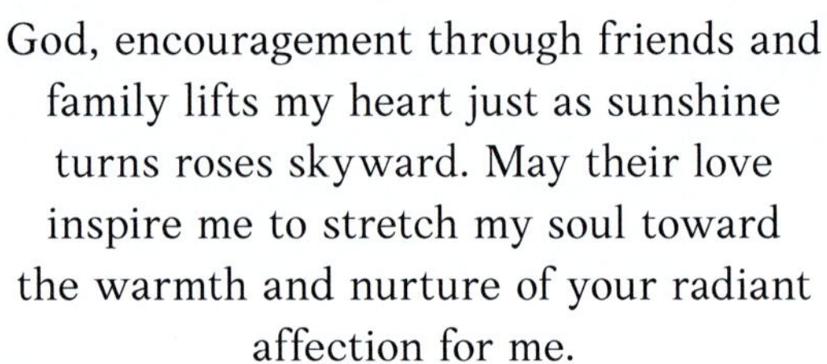

God, encouragement through friends and family lifts my heart just as sunshine turns roses skyward. May their love inspire me to stretch my soul toward the warmth and nurture of your radiant affection for me.

January 28

The obligation to live up to other people's expectations can be overwhelming, Lord. Sometimes I find myself trying to make everyone happy, though I know that's impossible. Here is your answer to my dilemma: You call me to greet every person with a heart of love. I may not be able to give them everything they want, but I can love them. Loving them will help me figure out the next step. If they are disappointed in what I have to offer, help me leave responsibility for their feelings with them and not carry false guilt. I am glad to do what you need from me, Father. What you ask of me is not a to-do list, but a way of relating that always extends your love.

January 29

Lord, when I see anger and strife around me, it's difficult to keep my own equilibrium and trust in you. I try to have faith that "all things work together for good to them that love God" (Romans 8:28), but my faith does falter. When I'm surrounded by division, let me be rooted in faith, unshaken by the passing concerns of this world. Let me be a person of peace myself—not false peace, that ignores problems that need to be addressed—but the true peace that comes from you.

January 30

Father in heaven, sometimes I feel anger welling up inside me, and I need to turn to you for counsel. Please stay near to me and help me to find ways to express my emotions without harming another's feelings or getting myself so upset I cannot see past my own feelings. I need to understand myself, express myself, and accept myself—all within the bounds of your teachings.

January 31

Dear heavenly Father, I truly want to do good toward others. I don't want to just talk about being good, but I desire to be more compassionate. God, I need for you to teach me to be far more sensitive to the needs and sorrows of the people you have placed in my life and to be kind and encouraging toward them. I need for you to teach me how to truly love. I pray for this with all my heart.

February 1

God, I take comfort in the knowledge that you will never give me more than I can handle. I do ask you though to give me the strength and courage to handle what you've given me. I am grateful to be alive, but I could use some help right now in dealing with these feelings of anxiety and doubt. Give me the promise of your everlasting comfort so I may take that with me no matter what dark or stressful path life takes me down. You will be the lamp that guides my steps and warms my heart.

February 2

Thank you, Lord, for helping us through our hard times. You have shown your love for us and made us more compassionate people. Help us show the same love to others who are going through hard times.

February 3

You don't need to have perfect pitch to sing praises to God. Many worshippers take great comfort in the psalmist's mandate to make a joyful noise to the Lord. Joyful noises from attuned hearts are music to God's ears.

February 4

Sometimes my heart is so overwhelmed, God, that I don't know where to begin my prayer. Help me to quiet my soul and remember that you know everything inside of my mind before I ever come to you with it. Still, I need to tell you about it, Lord, and I know you want me to tell you. Thank you for being such a faithful listener and for caring about everything that concerns me. When I remember that, it helps me slow down, take a deep breath, and begin the conversation.

February 5

Bless me with a peacemaker's kind heart and a builder's sturdy hand, Lord, for these are mean-spirited, litigious times when we tear down with words and weapons first and ask questions later. Help me take every opportunity to compliment, praise, and applaud as I rebuild peace.

February 6

Help me to see with new eyes today—especially the burden of care that others harbor within them. Grant me insight to see beyond smiling faces into hearts that hurt. And when I recognize the pain, Lord, let me reach out.

February 7

Lord, it is sometimes hard to love those around me when they are so different in their beliefs and behaviors. I find myself sometimes feeling intolerant, even afraid. But you gave me the commandment to love others as myself. I understand that if I love you then I love all of your creation. Help me to open my heart and my mind to those I see as being different, and find in them the common light of your presence.

February 8

My heavenly Father, what do I have to fear when you are the one caring for me? And yet, I do fear; irrationally I fear, despite your faithfulness, despite your assurances, and despite your promises. Why do I still fear? I don't always understand my trembling heart and the shadows of things far smaller than you before which it cowers. Please liberate me from these lapses of trust. Free me to stand fearlessly, supported by faith and hope, in the center of your great love for me.

February 9

I am here right now, Father, because I do want to walk in your ways. I know the key is staying connected to you because the ways of the world are all around me, always imposing a different set of values and a different worldview. Give me a wise and discerning heart in all things today so I can stay on track.

February 10

Sometimes when I am going through a hard time, I have friends or family members who are willing to offer help, to share my burden for a while, but I have a hard time accepting their help because I feel I should be strong and handle it alone. Father God, please help me balance independence and community. Please help me remember that part of being in a loving relationship is accepting love—that in accepting love, I accept you more deeply in my life, for you are love!

February 11

God, I do not intend to hurt you and others. I am not always sure what happens in those times when I do hurt you and others. I am thankful that you forgive. Please help others to forgive me, too. Remind us all to follow your teachings. We pray that you will guide and comfort us.

February 12

Touch and calm my turbulent emotions, God of the still waters. Whisper words to the listening ears of my soul. In hearing your voice, give me assurance beyond a shadow of a doubt that you are my companion in life, eternally.

February 13

I cry out to you, O Lord, from the belly of my fear. In this dark place of anxiety and confusion over health and future, I ask that you reach down and guide me into the light of day. My faith in you is strong, and my trust in you is steadfast. Come to my aid, O Lord, as you did when Jonah called to you.

February 14

Lord, the new command you gave your disciples, to love one another, is just what we need to challenge our children when they fight among themselves. We want to remind them that they're not showing their love when they quarrel, because love is kind, patient, and doesn't insist on its own way. Our thanks and praise to you, dear Father, for the tender messages from your word. May they take root and grow in our children's hearts.

February 15

Father, you are a God of love, compassion, and forgiveness. You have shown my family the right way to live in the world. You are a God my children can rely on to guide them and keep safe. What wonders you perform! Your power at work in us can accomplish more than our meager minds can even conceive. You boost our confidence and make us better than we are. In times of trouble, you find solutions we never could have imagined. Lord, we do not deserve your care and attention, but you give them anyway. For this we exalt you forever.

February 16

There seems to be every reason to give up and give in, steadfast God, for so many of my days are a struggling drudgery. When I falter, remind me that with you I am as resilient as crocuses blooming in the snow.

February 17

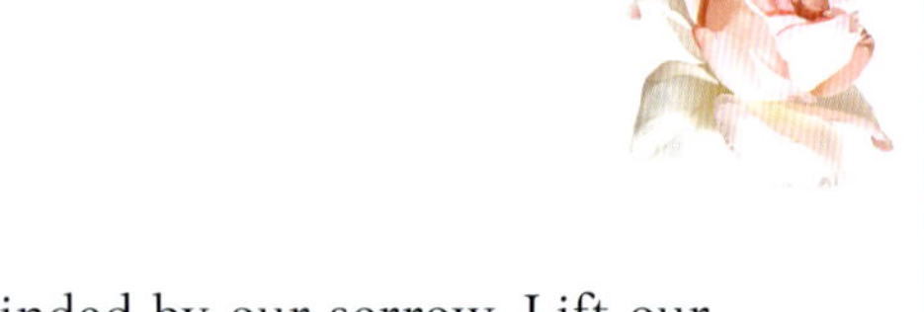

We are blinded by our sorrow. Lift our eyes and bless us, O Father, with a defiant hope, steadfast trust, and fire in the belly to emerge from this darkness victorious and whole once again, standing in the light you've given us.

February 18

Thank you for your wise ways, Lord. Following them fills my life with true blessings—the riches of love and relationship, joy and provision, peace and protection. I remember reading in your Word that whenever I ask for your wisdom from a faith-filled heart, you will give it, no holds barred. So I'll ask once again today for your insight and understanding as I build, using your blueprints.

February 19

O Lord, this aloneness is almost more than I can take! If I could escape in a good night's sleep, I would. But my thoughts and fears and emotions are restless, hovering around this center of heartache. If it were not for you being here with me, I would despair. But your quiet presence keeps me from unraveling. These nights, these long drawn-out nights of solitude, are where I find you waiting, ready to speak comfort to my heart and assure me that you have a future in store for me that is good and worth waiting for. Tonight, even if sleep eludes me again, I'll continue to rest in your love for me.

February 20

Bless us in this time of play together. Let each child know he or she is loved. And let us parents recognize that the love we offer here is the same affection you have already worked in our own hearts.

February 21

Security, loving God, is going to sleep in the assurance that you know our hearts before we speak and are waiting, as soon as you hear from us, to transform our concerns into hope and action, our loneliness into companionship, and our despair into dance.

February 22

How lovely, God, the newness of the life around me. Flower buds will soon be peeking out from many places. It's easy to imagine an angel behind every one breathing life and sending good energy to the world. Give me eyes to see. Give me a heart to respond.

February 23

Source of all life and love, let this family be a place of warmth on a cold night, a friendly haven for the lonely stranger, a small sanctuary of peace in the midst of swirling activity. Above all, let its members seek to reflect the kindness of your own heart, day by day.

February 24

Lord, your Word is so alive and so very powerfully vibrant that it almost seems like an illumination when I am reading it. When I am troubled, opening the Bible is like turning on a comforting light that dispels the darkness of a gloomy room. Thank you, Lord, for loving us so dearly that you gave us your wisdom to illuminate our lives.

February 25

Lord, you come to us in the storm, the fire, and even in the stillness of a quiet moment. Sometimes your message is strong, carried on bustling angelic wings; sometimes our spirits are nudged, our hearts lightened by the gentle whisper of spirit voices. However you approach us, your message is always one of tender love and compassion. Thank you for the certainty—and the surprise—of your holy voice.

February 26

Loving God, help us sense your angelic messengers whenever and wherever and however they come to us. In the darkness of winter, the brightness of spring, the abundance of summer, the transitions of autumn, may we expect to be visited by your heavenly beings. And when those visits happen, may our eyes be open and our gratitude heartfelt.

February 27

Gracious God, help us to learn from the children in our lives. Let us view the world with their innocent eyes and laugh joyously with them at the wonder of your creation. Make us mindful of others' hurts and sympathetic to others' needs. Open our hearts to the world, as children open themselves, with delight and curiosity, to all the world's experiences.

February 28

As we learn to trust you, God, we discover your strengthening presence in various places and people. Wherever we encounter shelter, comfort, rest, and peace, we are bound to hear your voice, welcoming us. And in whomever we find truth, love, gentleness, and humility, we are sure to hear your heartbeat, assuring us that you will always be near. Thank you, God.

March 1

God of my heart, sometimes I feel like a broken person. I do not know how to handle the suffering this life will often bring to me. I am not strong enough to do all of this alone. Be my strength, God, and do for me what I simply cannot do for myself. Be the glue that binds the pieces of my soul back together, and make me firm, that I may rise and step back upon the joyful path of life again.

March 2

Today has not been a horrible day, but it has not been a good one either. I've been snappish and irritable, having to work hard to be kind to my coworkers, patient with my children, loving to my spouse. There's no particular reason why—just one of those days. Lord, please let me act with love—with patience, with kindness, with self-control—even when I'm feeling small and petty.

March 3

How we love a good story, O Lord. Especially a story with hope and promise and a good ending. When it comes to your Word, give me an open ear so that I might hear your good news, an open mind ready to accept it, and an open heart willing to be transformed by your love and acceptance of me.

March 4

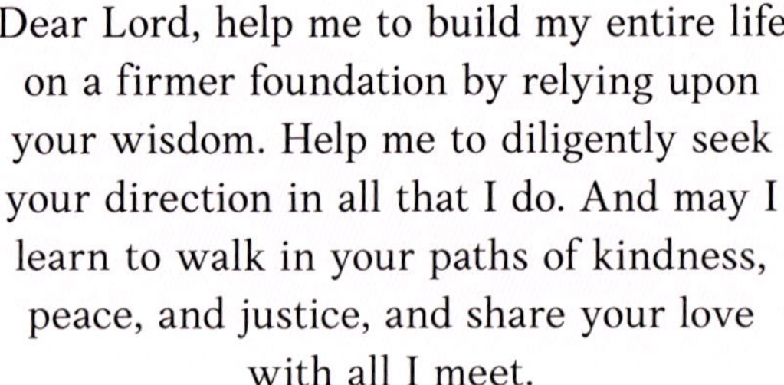

Dear Lord, help me to build my entire life on a firmer foundation by relying upon your wisdom. Help me to diligently seek your direction in all that I do. And may I learn to walk in your paths of kindness, peace, and justice, and share your love with all I meet.

March 5

Heavenly Father, talking to others about you isn't always easy. It's hard for me to express my emotions in mere words. Though I long to tell my children all you mean to me, self-consciousness gets in the way. Help me to speak to them from my heart. Inspire me with language that will fall on fertile soil. May I be like Moses as I teach my children about you, with words as welcome as the rain and dew on thirsty plants.

March 6

Merciful God, my heart is often heavy. In those times, visit me with angels, that I may receive the peace that comes only from you. And then, with the lightness of angelic wings, may I lift my face to heaven to receive your gift of new life.

March 7

Lord, I think I finally get it. You invest your spirit in me so that I can offer you to the world around me. Help me do this well. My hands and my heart should always be available to you, though I may not always feel up to the task.

March 8

Grace of my heart, I turn to you when I am feeling lost and alone. You restore me with strength and hope and the courage to face a new day. You bless me with joy and comfort me through my trials and tribulations, both small and great. You direct my thoughts, guide my actions, and temper my words. You give me the patience and kindness I need to be good. Grace of my heart, I turn to you.

March 9

God Almighty, thank you for the people that inspire me to accept others. Let me learn to love everyone—including myself.

March 10

Lord, I pray I can find a place within my heart where I can let go of worries. I want to be filled with the calmness of a faith in you.

March 11

Lord, we often think of peace as something that comes when we're ready, when our hands are folded and our minds quiet. But your love and presence are in all things in this world, the loud and the quiet, the raging river as well as the silent pond. You are everywhere, and it is as easy to hear you on a bustling city street as it is in the isolated silence of a redwood forest. Please remind me that I can find your comforting peace anywhere, if my eyes are open and my heart is willing.

March 12

When I was a child, I had my favorite blanket. I took that blanket everywhere, wrapping myself in its warmth and comfort. Now I am all grown up, and you, God, are the one I turn to for that warmth and comfort. Like that blanket, I know all I have to do is call you and you will wrap your love around me and make me feel safe and snug. I am your child still, and no matter how old I get, I will always need you watching over me and making sure I am happy and secure. For you, God, are my permanent security blanket, my safe harbor from the storm, my rock, my home.

March 13

Lord, put into my heart
a pure faith that is fit for heaven.

March 14

Bless me with patience and a steadfast heart to help me get through trying times. Heal the wounds of my heart and soul with the soothing balm of your comforting presence, that I may be able to always love.

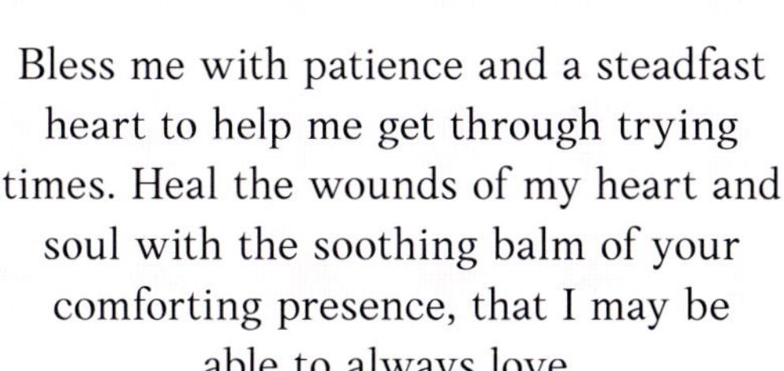

March 15

God, you have shown me light and life. You are stronger than any natural power. Accept the words from my heart that struggle to reach you. Accept the silent thoughts and feelings that are offered to you. Clear my mind of the clutter of useless facts. Bend down to me, and lift me in your arms. Make me holy as you are holy.

March 16

Lift up your heart in sweet surrender to the God who is waiting to shower you with blessings. Lift up your soul on wings of joy to the God who is waiting to guide you from the chaos of shadows out into the light of a peace that knows no equal.

March 17

Lord, teach me to love as you love for I know that is the only way I can show my gratitude for your love of me. Sometimes it's easy to love when all is going well. I need you when loving is not easy. It's hard to love when I'm tired and see no signs of relief; when the kids are demanding and totally selfish; when I just don't like what others are doing, even those closest to me. Enable me to love not because I feel like it but because that is what we are created to do and because it is the only way for there to be hope in this world.

March 18

Father, you are the greatest of all peacemakers. You made reconciliation with humanity possible by means of great personal sacrifice—but without compromising the truth. Show me how to follow your example today. Help me not to settle for fake peace—the kind that comes when lies are allowed to prevail for the sake of avoiding conflict. Instead, grant me the courage, grace, and wisdom to work toward real peace, which values all people and fulfills our need for truth and love.

March 19

Lord, sometimes I feel like we are all only living out a minuscule amount of the life you have offered us. Help us tap into your stream of living water on a regular basis. Teach us to live more courageously, love more extravagantly, and give more generously. We don't want life to pass us by. Keep us open to all you have wrapped up in this gift called life. And then one day, bring us into abundant life with you.

March 20

Holy God, even in times of fear and uncertainty, please remind me that you surround me always. With every breath I take, let me breathe in your merciful love. With every blink of my eyes, let me see your comforting presence. With every beat of my heart, let me feel your spirit envelop me. I ask that you make me yours, totally and completely, and let me rest in the loving refuge of your arms.

March 21

There is no greater comfort to a broken spirit than the love of God. There is no more soothing a balm to heal the wounds of a suffering soul than the love of God. There is no deeper peace to be found for a restless heart than the love of God.

March 22

Father, there are many events in our lives over which we have no control. However, we do have a choice either to endure trying times or to give up. Remind us that the secret of survival is remembering that our hope is in your fairness, goodness, and justice. When we put our trust in you who cannot fail us, we can remain faithful. Our trust and faithfulness produce the endurance that sees us through the tough times we all face in this life. Please help us to remember.

March 23

God, make me an open vessel
through which the waters of
your Holy Spirit flow freely.

March 24

Lord, with each breath I take I am aware that it is you who breathed life into me. My next breath is as dependent on you as my last breath was. And I can confidently rest in the knowledge that it will be you and you alone who will determine when the last breath leaves my body and I go to be with you.

March 25

Lord, today I want to give you thanks for all the little children who bring so much joy into the world. I feel that they must spring directly from your love for us. How we treasure the hugs and smiles of these little angels, Lord. They are as special to us as they are to you. Lay your hand upon their heads, Lord. Touch them with your grace, and keep them close to you.

March 26

Feelings of love tend to ebb and flow, Lord, and too often my actions are the result of my overly sensitive nature. Thank you for your love, which flows like a steady stream. Thank you for mercies that never dry up. Help my love to be more like yours today. Keep me from selfishly withholding or retracting it when I'm hurt, angry, or disappointed. Let love flow more—not less—where it seems most undeserved. Help me conquer the troubles around me by means of a flood of merciful love.

March 27

Sometimes it's good for me to just step back and look at the whole picture of who you are, Lord—to remember your greatness and meditate on all the implications of it. When I look at how big you are, my problems that seemed so gigantic a few moments ago suddenly seem almost silly. My big plans seem less important, and my high notions of myself get cut down to size. I come away not feeling diminished, though—rather lifted up in spirit and full of faith and gratitude. Surely we were made to praise you, Lord!

March 28

Lord, thank you for my pets—these angels who come to me in fluff and fur. Thank you for their magic of putting laughter in the hearts of those they love. Thanks for their trust and their unabashed desire to give affection and to be scratched behind the ears.

March 29

God, let the sorrow I experience in life wash over me like cleansing water. Let it rush over my rough-hewn heart and turn me into a smooth and polished stone, glistening in the sunlight.

March 30

Thank you, Lord, for reaching out and drawing me under your wings. Even though I am just one of billions of people who need you, your love is so great that you know my troubles, are concerned for my welfare, and are working to renew my dreams. I am so blessed to have you to turn to when I am faced with a calamity, and I am so very grateful that I have you to lean on. I praise you with all my heart.

March 31

God, when I am tired and just feeling down about everything in my life, your love reminds me that there is a spring of hope and renewal I can drink from anytime. It may take me awhile to come around, but I always come back to love as the reason to keep on going, even when my gas tank is empty. Love fuels me and gets me back out on the road of life, ready for whatever new challenge you have in store for me.

April 1

After a long winter, the first spell of warmer weather is a gift. We open the windows and though they first creak from disuse, soon fresh air enlivens the room. Our hearts quicken at the green scents of spring, at the promise of a new season and all the chapters yet to come. Opening our windows to a new time of year, we open our hearts and spirits.

April 2

The time of blooming flowers is coming! Lord, during this time of renewal when winter is turning to spring, thank you for shining your warm light upon us and holding out the promise of warmth and happiness to come.

April 3

I am grateful, God of Hope, for the gift of each new day, each new season, like the one unfolding around me now in flower, leaf, and birdsong, in seedling and bursting bud. When these events arrive as surely as dawn follows night and bloom follows bulb, I am uplifted by the fulfillment of your promise.

April 4

O Lord, how magnificent is your work in this world. We can stand at the seashore and feel our own souls rising and filling with your majesty as we marvel at the tides. Or we can walk down a trail and notice that each and every twig has been frosted individually with more icy flakes than we can imagine. We praise you for this awesome creation you share with us, Lord. The more we see of it, the more amazed we are. To you be the glory!

April 5

We praise you, Lord,
for eternal life. And we thank you for
your love for each one of us.

April 6

Dear Lord, in a busy life, I am grateful for those times when I can slow down. I turn off the news and put my technology away. I sit quietly, with or without a book, and become engaged with my surroundings. The rumble of a truck passing by. The spring smell of grass. A lampshade's soft glow. I am quiet, and my heart is full.

April 7

Lord, time and again I see that you intend for the generations to go through life together. The joy the youngest child brings to the eldest grandparent is such a blessing to all who witness it. Even when it isn't possible for us all to be together all the time, let us see the wisdom in sharing our lives. Please keep us ever alert to the unique gifts each generation has to share.

April 8

I look around and see so many people hurting one another, and it makes my heart heavy and sad. What kind of world are we creating for our children? Why must there be so much hatred and violence and inhumanity? I pray for a way to walk through this world without drowning in sorrow and defeat. I pray for a light to focus upon when all I hear and see is dark and bleak. Help me, God, to focus on the beauty and wonder the world has to offer. Help me recognize the good and the kind and the loving.

April 9

There's a saying that implies we should forgive and forget, but there are some things I just don't think I can forget. Certain people have hurt me deeply, and I don't want their toxic presence in my life anymore. I ask in prayer that you help me come to a place inside my heart where I can truly forgive them of their sins, and let go of them to make way for healing and peace. I no longer want to live in anger and regret, nor do I want to hold on to people who simply are not good for my happiness. Please show me the way to completely forgive, and then to lovingly close the door so that I can begin to become whole again.

April 10

When I think about your example of love, dear God, I realize that love is far more than a warm emotion. It is a deep commitment to look out for another's best interest, even at my own expense. Please teach me to put my pride and my heart on the line. Please protect me, Lord, as I love others in your name.

April 11

It's easy to praise you for your majesty and power when we see thundering waterfalls, crashing ocean waves, or majestic sunsets. Help us to learn to praise you when we see a dewdrop, a seedling, or an ant.

April 12

Praise the Lord, for he has seen the affliction and heard the groans of his people—both his children who were slaves in Egypt and those of us who have been in bondage to physical pain. Indeed, he has come to me in my darkest moment and rescued me from my misery. He is a compassionate and wonderful God. He loves his children and watches over each and every one of us.

April 13

Give me peace of mind today, for I am worried about so many things. Give me peace of heart today, for I am fearful of challenges before me. Give me peace of spirit today, for I am in a state of confusion and chaos. I ask, God, for your peace today, and every day, to help keep my feet on the right path and my faith solid and unmoving. Without peace, I don't see the answers you place before me. Without peace, I cannot hear your still, small voice within. Shower me today with your loving peace, God, and all will be well in my mind, heart, and spirit.

April 14

God, you promise to give wisdom to anyone who asks for it. This offer has only one condition: that we ask in faith, not doubting your promise. Well, since you're offering, I'm not going to be shy about asking. I need wisdom, and I need it today. Thank you for being generous with your gifts rather than giving them to only a select few. In fact, you make receiving them as simple as just asking. You never cease to amaze me with your generosity, Lord. I'm deeply grateful.

April 15

Creator God, I've been so busy with the obligations in my life that I've neglected my own creativity. I thought it was the right thing to do, but lately I've felt the urge to stretch my talents. Lord, please guide me. I feel guilty about wanting to do something for myself, but I think this will reduce my stress, and my spirit could use a little uplifting! You have given me many talents. Can I use them to renew my mind and spirit?

April 16

Guide us, dear God, to the perfect destiny you have set out for us. Help keep us on the path to right action, right choices, and right solutions to the problems we may encounter. Help deliver us from obstacles that may detour us and lead us astray. Show us the way to fulfill your divine plan.

April 17

Father God, in you I find comfort and peace after a day of working hard and pushing forward to reach my goals. In you I find strength when I've done all I can do on my own. In you I find my spirit renewed.

April 18

Lord, so often I keep doing the same things over and over and getting the same results. This is when I need for you to shine your light on my life and reveal to me all that I haven't been able to see through human eyes. You have all knowledge and every answer to the mysteries of the heavens and of this world. Show me, Lord. Give me just a bit more of the knowledge you possess.

April 19

Lord, I know that all of your commandments are important. I also know, though, that you once said your greatest commandment, after loving you, is for us to love one another. I think love is so important because so many other good things flow from love. If we love those around us, we will never do anything to hurt them. If you see our loving hearts in action, you can overlook and forgive any number of our more minor failures.

April 20

Lord, how much time do we spend looking into a mirror, and how often do we see you there? We were made in your image, but rather than focusing on that, we often focus on all the things we'd like to change. When others look at us, do they see our meager attempts to make our lips fuller and our eyelashes longer, or do they see the light of your love shining through our eyes? Teach us to focus less on our own appearance and concentrate more on presenting your face to those around us. It is you the world needs, not us.

April 21

Dear Lord, when I am sad, you give me hope. When I am lost, you offer me direction and guidance. When I am alone, you stand beside me. When my heart aches with sorrow, you bring me new blessings. Thank you for your gifts of grace, of love, and of healing.

April 22

I pray, Lord, for the ability to learn forgiveness. Often within my heart there is much that is negative. I pray to learn to let go of those feelings. I pray to learn to forgive others as I wish to be forgiven. I pray for the gifts of understanding and compassion as I strive to be more like you.

April 23

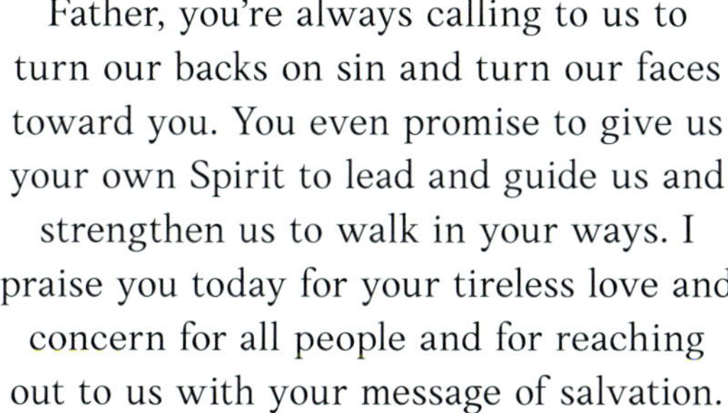

Father, you're always calling to us to turn our backs on sin and turn our faces toward you. You even promise to give us your own Spirit to lead and guide us and strengthen us to walk in your ways. I praise you today for your tireless love and concern for all people and for reaching out to us with your message of salvation.

April 24

Water that runs over moss-covered rocks: This is the sound of praise. Fingers that play upon ivory keys: This is the sound of worship. Silence that speaks even better than words: This is the sound of my thankful heart.

April 25

God gave the rainbow as a sign of his promise to never flood the entire world again. The colors that spread out in spectrum, as sunlight passes through water droplets in the sky, speak of God's faithfulness in keeping his promise to Noah and to all the generations that have followed. Faithfulness marks God's character. It is who he is, through and through. Let every rainbow we see remind us of God's faithful love, and let praise flow from our hearts to the one who always keeps his promises.

April 26

Lord, sometimes it's hard for us to discern the difference between brave, courageous actions and foolish, faulty ones. Often we rush ahead with a plan we think is from you only to watch it end in disaster. At these times we know we moved too fast. Yet we don't want to lack the faith to move forward when necessary! Give us wisdom and discernment, Lord. Let the courageous spirit you instilled in us fuel actions that bring you glory.

April 27

God of beasts and critters, bless all of my pets, for they bless me even when they shed on the couch and don't come back home when called. They love without strings and happily show us the simplest joys of walks and catnaps, slowing me to a pace you recommend.

April 28

May your eyes look kindly upon this family, Lord, for we need your love and guidance in our lives. This is a family that seeks to do the right things—to work hard for a living, to raise up children who will contribute to society, and to be a blessing in our neighborhood. But we know we need your constant help to do these things. May we be filled with love and happiness—all of us who live in this home: by fulfilling our responsibilities; by being accountable in all our actions; by giving whenever we can, even when it hurts; by nurturing warmth and understanding among us.

April 29

Lord, teach me to think ahead about the results my actions might inflict. If things go awry despite my forethought, help me admit my wrongs and right them.

April 30

Alleluia, Lord! How we praise you with our words, our songs, and our lives! When we look back over all the situations you've brought us through, we are so grateful. We are filled with confidence that we can face the future because you will be there with us. And so we just want to stop today and praise you for all you are and all you do!
Alleluia and Amen!

May 1

The Sun is shining and the breezes are blowing. Inspired by you, O God, I wisely invest in the future by deciding to chase kites on spring days, to chase balls on playgrounds, and to chase laughter rising from a baby's lips like bubbles on the wind rather than to chase dust bunnies beneath beds!

May 2

Heavenly Father, when you made the world, you were satisfied with the job and pronounced it "good." Because I am your child, I find satisfaction in creating, too. I give you thanks, Father, for the gift of creativity. Help me never to discourage but to encourage the sparks of creativity in others, so they can experience the pleasure of struggle and fulfillment in making something new. Only you can satisfy our longing souls by filling them with creative achievement.

May 3

Dear God, no one understands my suffering, but you do, for you know my heart even better than I do. Help me to walk through this dark valley of my pain and guide me back to the light of truth. I know that I am precious, but I don't feel that way right now. Help me see the reality of who I am—the magnificent creation you intended me to be.

May 4

Lord, I will do my best to remember that mistakes can actually have value. They show us the correct path to take next time.

May 5

Spirit, help me live one day at a time so that I may meet each day's challenges with grace, courage, and hope. Shelter me from the fears of the future and the anguish of the past. Keep my mind and heart focused on the present, where the true gifts of happiness and healing are to be found.

May 6

Lord, I need you to help me with the concept of forgiving people over and over again for the same behavior. I know you taught that there was no limit to the number of times we should forgive someone, but I get so weary of doing it, Lord. Help me to have a heart of forgiveness, so ready to forgive that I do so before the person who has wronged me even seeks my forgiveness. There's freedom in that kind of forgiveness, Lord. Help me claim it for my own.

May 7

Lord, when there seems to be no easy way out of a tough situation, I turn to you. When relationships seem too difficult to navigate, I turn to you. When I fear for my safety or feel threatened by bodily harm, I turn to you. You, O Lord, are my sanctuary. With you I am always safe. I praise you for this night and day!

May 8

We give thanks for your presence, which greets us each day in the guise of a friend, a work of nature, or a story from a stranger. We are reminded through these messengers in our times of deepest need that you are indeed watching over us. Lord, we have known you in the love and care of a friend, who comforts us and keeps us company in our despair. When we observe the last spring flower stretching faithfully to receive what warmth is left in the chilly sunshine, we are heartened and inspired to do the same. Lord, we are grateful receivers of all the angelic messages that surround us every day.

May 9

O Lord, your gift of love is often distorted in this world of ours. You are the source of the only perfect love we will ever know. Thank you, Lord, for abiding in us and helping us love ourselves and others. On this day, Lord, I pray that you will draw near to anyone who is feeling unloved. May they accept your unconditional love so they will know what true love is!

May 10

As hopeful spring approaches the glory of summer, I thank God for granting me good friends with whom I may share nature's bounty.

May 11

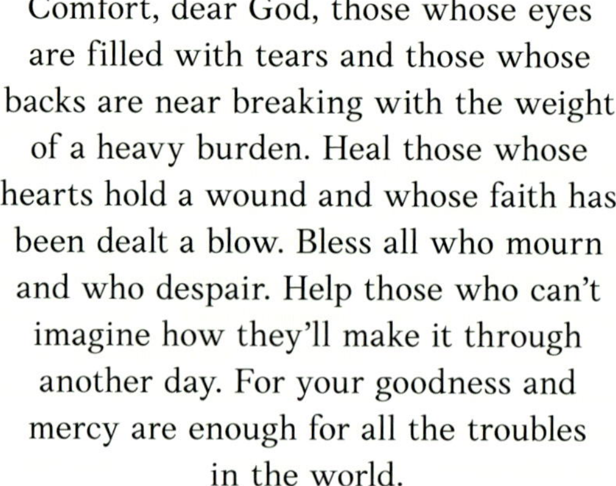

Comfort, dear God, those whose eyes are filled with tears and those whose backs are near breaking with the weight of a heavy burden. Heal those whose hearts hold a wound and whose faith has been dealt a blow. Bless all who mourn and who despair. Help those who can't imagine how they'll make it through another day. For your goodness and mercy are enough for all the troubles in the world.

May 12

God, I couldn't help noticing all the loveliness you placed in the world today! This morning I witnessed a sunrise that made my heart beat faster. Then, later, I watched a father gently help his child across a busy parking lot; his tenderness was much like yours. While inside a store, I spied an elderly couple. I could hear the man cracking jokes; their laughter lifted my spirits. Then early this evening, I walked by a woman tending her flower bed; she took great pleasure in her work, and her garden was breathtaking. Thank you, Lord, for everything that is beautiful and good in the world.

May 13

Victories, both big and small, are sweet when they come from you, God. Promotions, honors, breakthroughs, discoveries, and answered prayers—all come from you, and it's fun to savor them and know that your gracious hand has been actively providing for me. Help me remember to thank you when I taste victory today and to give you praise in all circumstances. My greatest reward in this life is your abiding presence with me.

May 14

Blessed Creator, thank you for the loving people in my life. Thank you for their open hearts and minds. Thank you for making them like you.

May 15

God, it's so hard to see your will in suffering. But while I can't understand your ways, I trust your heart. And so I cling to the faith that has sustained me through so many heartaches before, knowing that although it may be all I have, it's also all I need.

May 16

Lord, how we cling to your promise that the Holy Spirit is always near to all who believe in you. How comforting it is for us as parents to know that our children have the Holy Spirit to guide them and lead them into a purposeful life. We praise you, Lord, for your loving care for us and for our children and grandchildren.

May 17

You are the God of the stars and sky, trees and grass, fruit and flowers—the God of growing things. I offer my praise and gratitude for the quiet loveliness of my garden, where I can delight in the constant renewal of life. Help me to remember that though I plant and water, it is you who provides the life and growth.

May 18

Lord, how easy it is to express gratitude when times are good, but how difficult it can be for us to also thank you for the hard times—especially when we are in the midst of them. That's not wise of us, Lord, and we are sorry. For when we look back over all the ups and downs of our lives, we see that you were in fact working all things together for good. For lessons learned in the hard times, and for the strength you gave us to get through them, we give you thanks.

May 19

Dear God, what joy we have in gathering to pray and praise you together. How encouraging it is to share what's happening on our separate life journeys and see your hand at work in so many different ways. Thank you for arranging those times of fellowship, Lord.

May 20

Lord, no matter what we bring of ourselves to give you, even if we include all our hopes and dreams, it's never enough to give in return for all you've given to us. And so we give you our praise. We sing to you and come before you with our meager offerings, praying all the while that you will make something marvelous of them.

May 21

Today, heavenly Father, you may call upon me to listen to someone and hear that person's heart. It may be someone who needs to feel significant enough to be heard, or perhaps someone who is lonely and longs to be connected to another person, or maybe someone who is hurting and needs a sympathetic ear. Whatever the case, Lord, please open my ears so I may listen to someone today.

May 22

Lord, please bring this truth home to my heart today: that the essence of God is love—your love reaching us and setting our hearts aglow with love for you and for all people. Let love rule this day. Let love rule my heart. Help me enjoy living successfully in your wonderful love.

May 23

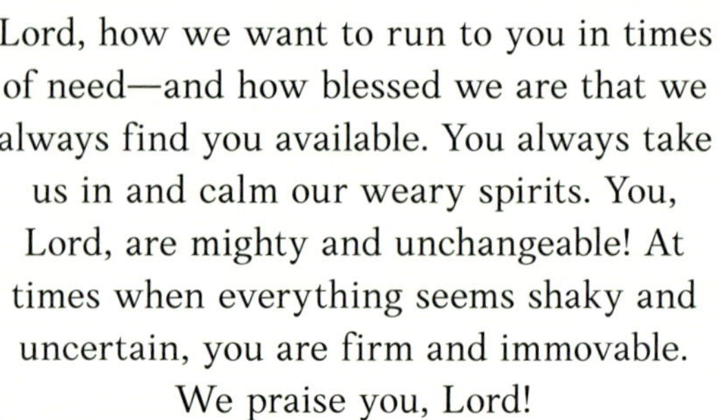

Lord, how we want to run to you in times of need—and how blessed we are that we always find you available. You always take us in and calm our weary spirits. You, Lord, are mighty and unchangeable! At times when everything seems shaky and uncertain, you are firm and immovable. We praise you, Lord!

May 24

Lord, I just want to tell you how much I love you and how grateful I am that you have taken me into your care. Ever since I've entrusted myself to you, you've kept me from becoming entangled in the kinds of things that would bring me to ruin. You fill my heart and mind with peace as I stay close to you. It's a miracle of your grace that I am standing tall today, lifting my praise to you from a heart full of love.

May 25

In your wisdom, you designed us to reject the word "don't." Like all your children, mine do better with "do" words. Do love, share, work, tend, tolerate, obey, forgive. Help me say "do" as often as I can. Let me be a positive example of your vision.

May 26

Today I give grudging thanks for the challenges in my life: the difficult cousin with whom I must learn to get along; the work project outside my wheelhouse; the stubborn tub drain that refuses to unclog. Life's trials teach me patience and they help me grow. I do not always like challenge, but I am a better person for it!

May 27

Lord, today I want to praise you for giving me the faith to believe, for faith itself is a gift from you. I lift up to you today all those I know who are having trouble accepting your gift of salvation. Be patient with them, Lord. Reveal yourself to them in a way that will reach them, and draw them into relationship with you. Our lives are incomplete without you, Lord. Send your grace to those who are struggling.

May 28

Lord, it's hard to count your blessings when all around you is chaos and despair. Though my heart is heavy and my mind cluttered, please help me to realize that before a flower can show its beauty to the Sun, it first is a seed buried in the dirt. Help me to stand above the negative things in life and cast my eyes instead upon the positives that are always there, like the seedling, growing toward the moment when it will appear above ground, face to the Sun.

May 29

God, I ask for a bold and courageous faith to get me through these trials and tribulations. Let me stand on my own feet, but steady my footing with the knowledge of your presence. Give me the strength of will to never give up, no matter how crazy life gets.

May 30

Lord, although we are often not certain of your intentions when you present us with unpleasant circumstances, we understand that you do have a reason. The hurt isn't just to spite us. Please help us to keep our outlooks positive and allow us to aid others who are as dismayed and in just as much pain as we are.

May 31

Lord, we praise you for all the beauty and wonder you've placed in the world. How creative of you to think of a creature as exuberant and joyful as the hummingbird! How interesting that you sprinkled spots on the backs of the newborn fawns that follow along behind their mother through our backyard. Let us never become so accustomed to your glorious creation that we take it for granted, Lord. You've blessed us with a wonderland, and we thank you for it.

June 1

Bless this food. And let it remind us once again that the soul, like the body, lives and grows by everything it feeds upon. Keep us drinking in only the good and the pure, for your glory.

June 2

Give me a hint, steadfast God, about what lies ahead, for I want to see around the corner to the future. If that's not possible, help me live as if the future is now, assured that each day's grace will be sufficient.

June 3

Creation shouts to me, Lord, about how amazing you are. I see the wonder of your wisdom in everything from the solar system to how bodies of water feed into one another to the life cycles of all living creatures. Everywhere I turn there is something that makes me think about how creative and insightful you are. Thank you for this universe that speaks without words. I hear it loud and clear, and it tells me of your magnificence.

June 4

Lord, if I were to boil down all the good news in the universe and look to see what I'd ended up with, there would be the eternal realities of your goodness, your love, and your faithfulness. And in this world, I don't have to look far for them—family, food, shelter, clothing, seasons, tides, moon, stars, life, beauty, truth, salvation. And that's just a sampling, a preview of a much longer list. I'm moved to praise you and to tell you how much I love you back.

June 5

You invented work, God, and I am grateful. Framer of the Cosmos, you've given me a project, too. Creator of all the things we see and know in this universe, sustain my hands to do it right.

June 6

Lord, you have seen each time when I've been abandoned by those in whose love I have trusted. You have known the loneliness in my soul. I must confess to you that it causes me to wonder if your love has failed me, too. I need you to assure me that you are still here and that you will always stay with me.

June 7

When grief fills my heart, Father, whether I'm feeling loss, shame, betrayal, or some other sorrow, I know it's temporary, even though at times it feels as though it will never go away. I know that your future for me is joy, and when it comes, I will not reject it. Strengthen me with your joy today, Father. I need it to lift up my soul.

June 8

God, bless me in my solitude.
I know that my character is what I am
in the dark, when no one is watching
and no one can see me.

June 9

Lord, my heart was broken, but I know
you can fix it. As I learn to depend on
you, give me the same thing you gave
your servant David: strength and a song.

June 10

Lord, in your infinite wisdom you knew we would need instruction for life, and so you placed in your Word the guidelines for living a productive life that brings you glory. Your Word nurtures us body and soul and keeps our minds focused on the beautiful, positive aspects of life. Thank you, Lord, for not leaving us here without a guidebook. We'd be lost without your Word.

June 11

Lord, so often it isn't until after a crisis has passed that we can see all the ways that you were present in the midst of it. Forgive us for focusing on the negative and missing your positive contributions. Remind us to expect your involvement—to actively watch for it, even! We need to be alert to the working of your Spirit in all things and give thanks at all times.

June 12

Dear God of comfort, I sense your loving presence all around me, in the ground beneath my feet, in the warming sunlight on my shoulders, in the gentle songs of the birds. You have made this world for us, your children, and the sight, sound, and touch of your creations comfort me as they surround me each day. Nothing can separate me from the joys of eternal life in you, just as nothing can separate me from the love you have shown for us in Jesus Christ.

June 13

In silence I kneel in your presence—bow my heart to your wisdom; lift my hands for your mercy. And open my soul to the great gift: I am already held in your arms.

June 14

Knowing he needs encouragement, I pray for my friend, Lord. Lifting my heart to you on his behalf, may I not fail, either, to reach my hand to his—just as you are holding mine.

June 15

Living in difficult times requires us to maintain a positive, hopeful attitude about the future. Having hope is vital for our mental, physical, and spiritual health. Lord, help me move into the future with a steadfast spirit, looking forward in faith and hope and trusting in the promises you have made to your people. Today I make a covenant to you that I will choose hope. If I encounter disappointment, I will choose hope. In the face of fear, I will choose hope. If I sense doubt washing over me, I will choose hope. Instead of giving in to sadness or despair, I will choose hope.

June 16

Comfort me, O God, as I seek shelter from the storms of everyday life. I am grateful for the good I have, but sometimes feel I cannot carry the burden of life's challenges alone. Remind me with your loving presence that no matter what my day brings me, you are there for me, with me, and on my behalf, making smooth the way before me. In your love I find rest.

June 17

Lord, do I value your love more than I value my paycheck? Do I crave it and savor it like I do chocolate? Do I consider it in my mind, pondering how insightful, how wise, how wonderful your works and ways are? Train my heart and mind to love your Word—to grasp all the depths of it and hold it close to my heart as the great treasure that it is.

June 18

Lord, thank you for calling me to yourself and then giving me your Spirit to strengthen me—heart, soul, mind, and body—to work in ways that bring honor to you. This goal of being a model of good works in every respect makes me realize how much I need you each moment. And as I grow in a life of doing what is right and true and good, help me grow in humility as well, remembering that you are the source of my strength.

June 19

Move our hearts with the calm, smooth flow of your grace. Let the river of your love run through our souls. May my soul be carried by the current of your love, towards the wide, infinite ocean of heaven. Stretch out my heart with your strength, as you stretch out the sky above the world. Smooth out any wrinkles of hatred or resentment. Enlarge my soul that it may know more fully your truth.

June 20

God, please remind me throughout my day that the moment is all I have in which to live. I can't retrieve or retract anything I've done or said just ten minutes ago. Nor can I be sure of what will happen ten minutes hence. So I pray, Lord, help me leave the past and the future with you so that I can experience the peace of your love in this important bit of eternity called "now."

June 21

Lord, how grateful I am for the wise leaders who came before me. Reading old journals, books, and accounts of their lives, I see how you were as active in their lives as you are in ours today. Reading about the past gives us hope and innovation for the future, and we come away reassured that you are always with us. Thank you, Lord, for your steadfast love through all generations.

June 22

Lord, how we thank you for the gift of laughter! Even in the midst of grief you send those happy memories that make us laugh and bring comfort to our souls. Laughter is so healing, Lord. It's reassuring to see so much evidence of your sense of humor.

June 23

I love being part of your flock, Lord. I could go on all day about your good care for me, and I often see evidence of how well you care for all the other members of your flock as well. You care for us as no one else ever could. You send us constant reminders that there is nothing you would withhold from us—not even your own life—to keep us safe in your love.

June 24

God, sometimes I wish I could be saved from the struggle and pain of learning the hard way. But, Lord, that's not your plan, and I need to be willing to wait as you work gently from the inside out. Please grant me some strength in this time of uncertainty. I trust and love you.

June 25

Lord, sometimes I fall so low that I feel ashamed and unworthy of being in your presence. At these times, remind me that it is never too late to throw myself at your feet and beg for your forgiveness and mercy. You are all good and all powerful, and your love for us never wavers. I can become whole and joyful again through you.

June 26

Lord, we stand in awe of your great sacrifice for us. Your journey to the cross is the reason we are free from the destruction of sin. It's why we can be forgiven and be united with you throughout eternity. No sacrifice is too great in response to your love for us. Keep us ever mindful, Lord. Keep us ever grateful.

June 27

Lord, even when the storm is raging all around me, I feel your still, comforting presence. Thank you for letting me know that no matter how dark the skies and regardless of how high the water rises, you are always with me. You meet me in the midst of the storm, wherever you find me, and you calm my troubled spirit. And so, Lord, I praise you in this storm. For in it, I find you.

June 28

Lord, I know I encounter them every day: your loved ones who are—on their own strength—desperately trying to make some sense out of this life. Help me reach out to them. Give me the words to say and the gentle approach that will lead them to the knowledge of your love and to the immense blessings you want to bestow on them.

June 29

What a relief in this throwaway world of ever-changing values to know that you, O God, are the same yesterday, today, and tomorrow. Your trustworthiness and desire for all your children to have good things never varies. You are as sure as sunrise and sunset.

June 30

God, help me celebrate this day with all my heart, to rejoice in the beauty of its light and warmth. May I give thanks for the air and grass and sidewalks. Help me feel grateful as others flow into my soul. May I cherish the chance to work and play, to think and speak—knowing this: All simple pleasures are opportunities for praise.

July 1

Lord, it's hard for me to conceive of how thoroughly you forgive me when I confess my sins to you. The stains on my soul are washed away, and you give me a fresh, clean start. Even though it's hard for me to wrap my understanding around this, please help me wrap my faith around it so I can believe that you completely forgive me.

July 2

You listen as a hearer of my heart.
And this is a moment to remind myself:
Prayers have never needed words.

July 3

Lord, thank you for this day! Let me treat this not just as any other day, but as a special gift. I ask that you open my eyes today to all the instances of grace around me. Let me take a special delight in the splendor of your creation. Let me see the best in people today. Let me see even the people who get my back up with your eyes, the eyes of love.

July 4

Gracious Father, I have often asked myself this question: How do I make my home a place of joy? A place where all who live here can relax and be happy? Now I know—the answer lies with you, O Lord. Like St. Augustine, our hearts are restless until they find their home in you. Joy begins when we let you into our lives. Life seems steadier, brighter, friendlier, safer. Your presence fills us with music. We make joyful noises when we sing your praises. All thanks to you, precious Lord, for our happy home. I will sing to you as long as I live.

July 5

Lord, I often pray for others when I need to pray with others. Show me the power of shared prayer as I meet with others in your name and in your presence.

July 6

Dear God, thank you for the powerful gift of friendship. May I tap into your strength to be steadfast and true to my friends; as Elisha accompanied Elijah, may I walk beside my friends in good times and bad.

July 7

Lord, it often happens that you are trying to communicate an important truth to us, but we are so busy searching for the truth elsewhere that we don't stop and listen. Teach us the importance of being still, Lord. Only when we are still can we be aware of your presence and hear your voice. Only when we quiet the stirrings of our own souls can we connect with your will! Speak to us, Lord—and help us be ready to listen.

July 8

I feel an old familiar panic coming over me, Lord. Comfort me now. As I breathe deeply, fill me with the knowledge that you are present and you are in control. Thank you, Lord. Only your intervention can calm my troubled soul.

July 9

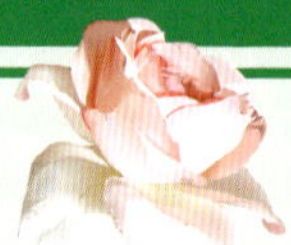

We enjoy too much the superior feeling of helping those in need. Teach us, Lord, that it can be much harder to receive than to give. And let us be humble enough to open our own hands, too, when we're clearly in need.

July 10

My biggest fear, God, is that in loving people who oppose you, I will have failed to stand against the injustices they have perpetrated against the defenseless ones they have harmed. How do I stand for justice and yet still love your enemies? Does my love cloak their iniquities? I know in my soul that I must love those people, but still, God, I wonder and fear that love is too easy. Strengthen me to love them, and give me wisdom to know how to extend your love without compromising your justice.

July 11

I feel an old familiar panic coming over me, Lord. Comfort me now. As I breathe deeply, fill me with the knowledge that you are present and you are in control. Thank you, Lord. Only your intervention can calm my troubled soul.

July 12

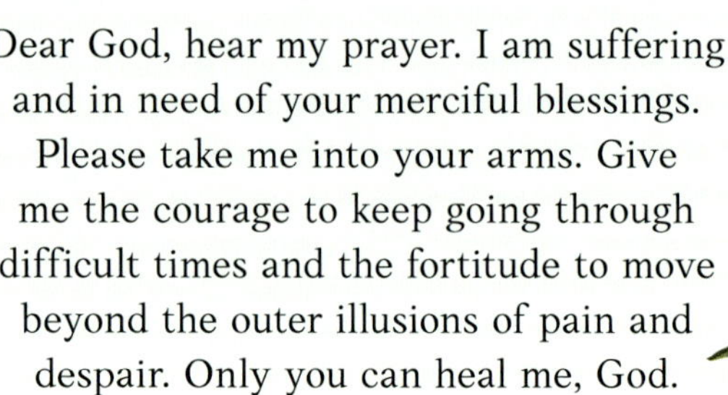

Dear God, hear my prayer. I am suffering and in need of your merciful blessings. Please take me into your arms. Give me the courage to keep going through difficult times and the fortitude to move beyond the outer illusions of pain and despair. Only you can heal me, God.

July 13

When feelings are hurt, Wise Physician, we curl in on ourselves like orange rinds, withholding even the possibility of reconciliation. Help us open up to new possibilities for righting wrong and sharing love without reservation, as the orange blossom offers its fragrance, the fruit of its zesty sweetness.

July 14

Help me understand, Lord, that the courage I am praying for is not dry-eyed stoicism and perky denial. Courage is not hiding my feelings, even from you, and putting on a brave false face. Rather it is facing facts, weighing options, and moving ahead. No need to waste precious time pretending.

July 15

When the winds of change and challenge blow into my life, I will take refuge in you, O Lord. When the darkness descends upon my house and home, I will fear not, for I will place my faith in you, O Lord. When my child is ill or my spouse is hurt, I will remain steadfast, for I know that you will be right there by my side, O Lord. Although I cannot see you, I know you are always with me, O Lord, and in that I take great comfort.

July 16

God, I feel happy today, and I have you to thank for that. No matter what is going on outside of me, I am strong and safe and secure inside because you love and care for me. Thank you for loving me when I have been cranky, tired, lazy, and even mean. Thank you for being there when I ignored your presence, God. Your steadfast love is a constant reminder of just how good I have it in life. And that makes me happiest of all!

July 17

Heavenly Father, when I was young, I thought all things hurt or broken could be fixed: knees, feelings, bicycles, tea sets. Now I've learned that not everything can be repaired, relieved, or cured. As a mother comforts her child, heal my hurting and grant me the peace I used to know. This I pray.

July 18

I am feeling my way in this darkness, God, and it seems I'm going in circles. Yet you have a way of reminding me in these quiet and calm moments that I am encircled by your love. With every move in any direction, I go no closer to you—nor farther either—than I already am.

July 19

Lord, give me the faith to take the next step, even when I don't know what lies ahead. Give me the assurance that even if I stumble and fall, you'll pick me up and put me back on the path. And give me the confidence that, even if I lose faith, you will never lose me.

July 20

When the pressures of
everyday life become too much,
God is there. God is always there.

July 21

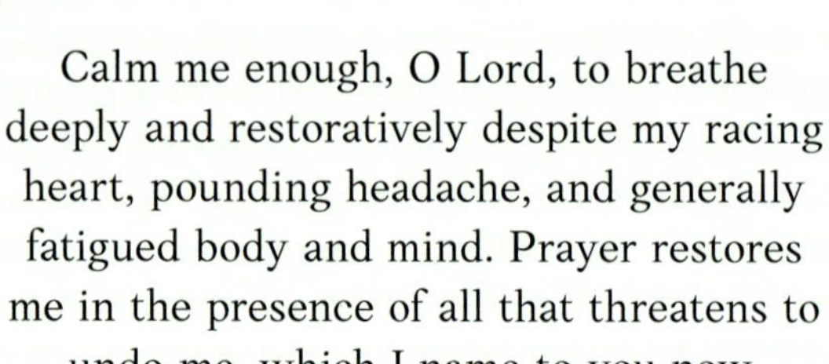

Calm me enough, O Lord, to breathe deeply and restoratively despite my racing heart, pounding headache, and generally fatigued body and mind. Prayer restores me in the presence of all that threatens to undo me, which I name to you now.

July 22

It's hard to face the day with hope, love, and faith when all I see on the morning news are stories of death and violence. Even if I don't watch, I hear about it from friends or see it on social networks and at my workplace. I pray for a powerful faith to hold onto as I try to understand why there is so much pain and suffering in the world. I pray for a steadfast awareness of your presence, and that there is a bigger picture behind the smaller pieces of life I see. Only you, Lord, know what that bigger picture is. I pray for the trust and the faith to live my life in love and light, despite any darkness around me.

July 23

Dear Father, I know you sent your Son to us to be our Lord. You sent your Son to watch over us. You sent your Son to bring us comfort, strength, hope, and healing when our hearts are broken and our lives seem shattered. We will never be alone, not when you are here with us always and forever. Remind us that we may look to you for strength.

July 24

In the times when I wait for pain or loneliness to pass, Great Comforter, cradle me as the wailing, lost child I've become. Closing my eyes and breathing deeply, I feel your warming presence as a blanket tossed around my shoulders and know that no matter how lost I feel right now, you hold the most important truth, whispering it now: "You are my beloved child. I am with you."

July 25

Good morning, God! We greet you with our many morning faces. We arise sometimes grumpy, sometimes smiling, sometimes prepared, sometimes behind. Always may we turn to you first in our family prayer. Bless us today and join us in it.

July 26

An anchor digs into the seabed and prevents the ship from drifting due to wind or current. We have an anchor like that, holding us sure and steadfast. With all the shifting currents and winds in our day, our sure hope is that which anchors us to the unchanging purpose and power of God. That hope keeps our souls from drifting away or crashing into a rocky shore. Thanks be to God.

July 27

When twelve-year-old Melissa found herself suddenly courted by the “cool girls” in her middle school, she began to ignore an old friend, Lily. Lily called her out on it, but Melissa’s new friends laughed and said Lily wasn’t worth Melissa’s time. Feeling torn and unhappy, Melissa talked to her mom, who encouraged her to talk to God; in the quiet of home and prayer, Melissa saw the situation, and her steadfast friend, with clarity. Dear God, a good friend lets us know when we’ve done wrong. May I be open to words of constructive criticism, shared by those who love me; may I see false platitudes for what they are.

July 28

Lord, thank you for bringing other people into our lives to help us heal. We appreciate how much they aid us. Please remind us to thank them for reaching out to us. Thank you for extending your love to us through them.

July 29

Father, unity among your people is precious to you—and precious to us as well. We cannot achieve it without your assistance, though. Help us to keep petty disagreements from dividing us. Give us the grace to work through any disagreement with love and understanding.

July 30

I admit that the slightest distraction can pull my mind out of its orbit around you, Father. You know how I am: I can be praying or praising you one minute, and the next moment a phone call with some disturbing news or a careless driver cuts me off and POOF!—my peace has left the building, and I'm all out of sorts. I want to ask you, though, to help me. I want to grow into a more steadfast frame of mind—one that can take bad news and thoughtless people in stride, acknowledging them for what they are, but not allowing them to rattle my world. Would you help me take a step in that direction today?

July 31

God, you are my rock and my solid foundation. When the storms of life rage around me, I know that I can seek warmth and security in your loving grace. You are a beacon guiding me through the thick fog of fear and confusion to the safe comfort of the shore. Steady and true are your love and your strength. Steadfast and secure am I in the light of your changeless and timeless presence that permeates the darkest of nights.

August 1

What a wonderful day! And now, God of rest and peace, the children are sleeping, replete with the joys of our summer discoveries that they are savoring to the last drop. We celebrate the joy of ordinary days and rest in your care.

August 2

Thank you God for leaving the Sun on longer in the summer so we can play more.

August 3

Maker of us all, help us to appreciate the gifts of the world's children: those we see daily, those who live all across the globe, and those whose angelic spirits touch us from another time.

August 4

Coming together in worship with prayer, song, and psalm makes us expectant people. Here we find what we came seeking: your abiding, ever-present, unconditional, daily love. We leave, blessed with the truth that it goes with us into the rest of our lives.

August 5

Time is tight, Lord, and I wonder why I bother to pray. The question is answer enough: I need a relationship where I don't have to bluff and hurry. And when I pray boldly? I offer myself as a possible answer to prayer.

August 6

God, today I ask you for more strength—not just for myself, but for the others I care about. There are many couples that need strength to get past conflicts in their relationships. Cover them with your overwhelming love. There are teenagers, still figuring out who they are, who need the strength to withstand temptations. Shore up their growing souls. There are single parents working night and day to provide for their families. Guard their health and refresh their energy. There are elderly citizens who need strength to do the things they easily used to do. Give them grace to live mightily for you. All around me are people with emotional wounds and spiritual struggles, those who feel ill-equipped, exhausted, and overwhelmed. Support them with your power for your eternal glory.

August 7

Love indeed makes the world go around and nothing compares to your love. My prayers today are not just for myself, but for all living things, that we may all feel a little more loved, a little more cherished. So many of us go through life thinking we don't matter. I pray your love awakens those in need to truly understand, as I do, that every single one of us is precious in your sight. I pray love wins over hate and lightens every dark corner. I pray love dominates the hearts of humans and erases hatred and division. I pray your love serves to bring us together and close the gaps of differences and separation. Love is the greatest miracle, Lord, and I am grateful to experience your love daily.

August 8

Lord, my lips praise your name and I sing to the heavens! I rejoice in your power. I hold you above all others, for I know that you can cure all ailments, comfort all hurts, remove all sins, and conquer all enemies. You are the source of all that is powerful and right, and all good flows from you alone. You are my redeemer, my savior, my protector, and my solace, for now and evermore.

August 9

Everything looks much brighter than it did before. My prayer for strength has been answered. My cries for help have been heard. My pleas for mercy flew directly to your throne. Now I'm ready to help my neighbor, Lord. Let me not delay.

August 10

Lord, we've tossed our prayers aloft, and hopefully, expectantly, we wait for your answers. As we do, we will: listen for you to speak in the voice of nature; see you as a companion in the face and hand of a friend; feel you as a sweet-smelling rain or a river breeze; believe you can provide encouragement, direction, and guidance for those who have only to ask. We feel your presence.

August 11

Lord, I pray for a strong spirit to stand against my fears today. I don't ask for fearlessness, because I do feel fear, and I do worry and doubt and I am human. Instead, I pray that you will be at my side in frightening situations, and that you will never leave me abandoned and forgotten. I pray you will shore up my own spirit and give me a sharp mind and deep faith, so that I can overcome any blocks in the road to love, peace, and happiness. Lord, stand beside me, and hold my hand, but also give me that extra bit of courage for the times you ask that I walk through the darkness alone.

August 12

When I am thankful for what I have, I am given more. When I am not thankful, what I have is taken away. Gratitude is like a door that, when opened, leads to even more good things. But to be ungrateful keeps that door closed, and keeps me away from what God wants to bless me with. I am thankful, always.

August 13

Excuse me, God, but it's pretty dark in here right now. If it's not too much trouble, I could sure use an angel or two to help me see what's going on. Just a little help to get me moving in the right direction would be so very much appreciated. I know the dawn is coming, I'm just not sure which direction to turn to find it.

August 14

I love the freedoms I enjoy as your child, Father. I also deeply appreciate the freedoms I enjoy as a citizen of a free country. Both citizenships—my heavenly one and my earthly one—call for responsible living on my part, but these responsibilities are really a joy and a privilege. Help me to always keep this in the forefront of my mind as I make choices each day.

August 15

Lord, if all the prayers ever prayed were linked together, surely they would reach to heaven and back countless times! We want to be a people who pray without ceasing, Lord. Hear both the prayers we utter and the silent prayers of our hearts, and may you also sense how grateful we are to serve a God who listens to our prayers and sends us his answers.

August 16

Lord, I know my friend is overwhelmed right now. Just as you lift my burdens when I come to you in prayer, show me what I can do to make her load lighter. I lay her troubles before you, Lord. I know our efforts can lift her burdens.

August 17

You heard my prayers to ease my pell-mell race through life, and I am changing. Only you could teach this old dog new tricks. I feel your companionship in walks and exercise, in contemplation and prayer. I'm enjoying this new pace you set.

August 18

Give thanks to God, for he is good. Even when we are struggling, God is there to help us. Even when we are feeling lost and alone, God stands beside us and shows us we are loved. Even when we are sure we cannot go on, God picks us up and carries us. Give thanks to God.

August 19

Thank you for those who pray for me, Father. Thank you for putting me in their hearts and minds. I know that at times someone is keeping me in their prayers, and I haven't the faintest clue. It could be my hairdresser, chiropractor, pastor, or even someone I've just met. Perhaps a checker at the grocery store recalls a bit of conversation we had and now prays for me from time to time. You work in such unusual ways that I never know how it might be happening—I just know that it is so, and I am grateful.

August 20

Lord, as I walk in your spirit of strength and love today, may others see what life in you is like. It isn't mere religion or a list of rules and regulations. Rather, it's real life full of adventure, challenge, wonder, joy, and peace—all in the context of relationship with you as I live through the energy you provide. Thank you for the spirit of boldness that enables me to live out my faith without fear.

August 21

Lord, how many times have I resolved to spend time first thing each morning in your Word and in prayer—and how many times have I neglected to do so! A day that begins with you, Lord, is sure to be a day blessed by you. Give me an insatiable thirst for time with you, Lord.

August 22

Lord, how precious water is to us, and how parched and desperate we are when it's in short supply. How grateful we are that you promise us access to the living water that will never run dry! Keep us mindful of that refreshing supply today.

August 23

Lord, how grateful I am that you are willing to go before me to prepare the way. Even when I sense that a new opportunity is from you and has your blessing, I've learned I still need to stop and ask you to lead before I take the first step. Otherwise I will stumble along in the dark, tripping over stones of my own creation! Everything goes more smoothly when you are involved, Lord.

August 24

May I wake up in the morning and be grateful for the new day ahead. Every 24 hours is an opportunity to live life more fully, and love more deeply. May I look at each moment and see the gift it brings. May I cherish the present as it unfolds. And, when I go to sleep at night, may I be thankful for the experiences God gave you. This is a life lived well.

August 25

Lord, you said to first seek your kingdom and all else will be given me. I tried for so long to seek those outer things first; those material things I thought would make me happy. And all it left me was feeling lost and alone and cold. But the kingdom you offer is one of love, mercy, and everlasting comfort. Your wisdom is far more precious than rubies and more priceless than gold. I understand that all good things can come to me only when I first immerse myself in your loving presence. That thought brings me a comfort nothing outside of me ever could.

August 26

God, I am hurting today. All the wounds I've received in this lifetime seem open and raw, and only the balm of your love can comfort me. I need you to take me in your hands, fill me with your sweetness, and ease all the aching, lonely places as only you can. I know that your power is endless and your love is merciful, and I have faith in your all-healing presence. I pray that all my worries and cares will be washed away from me.

August 27

When we grieve for lost loved ones, we grieve for ourselves. Let us celebrate that those who have gone home to heaven now know the full essence of God's true love.

August 28

Prayer, O God, is as steadying as a hand on the rudder of a free-floating boat and as reliable as sunrise after night. It keeps me going, connected as I am to you, the source of wind beneath my daily wings.

August 29

I confess, Lord, that in my haste to come to you in prayer and to present my daily laundry list of requests, I forget the other side of prayer. I forget to listen for your answer. I know that if I am patient enough, your gentle message will come to me when I wait for it.

August 30

Dear God, complaints sometimes come first before I can feel free to love you. Sometimes you seem distant and unreasonable, uncaring. Help me understand why life can be so hurtful and hard. Hear my complaints and, in the spirit of compassion, show me how to move through pain to rebirth.

August 31

Held up to your light, our broken hearts can become prisms that scatter micro-rainbows around us. Our pain is useless as it is, redeeming God, just as a prism is a useless chunk of glass until light passes through it. Remind us that the smallest sunbeam in a shower can create a rainbow. Use our tears as the showers and your love as the Sun. Looking up, we see the tiniest arches of hope in the lightening sky.

September 1

Lord, I know that it was not David's sling that won the victory against Goliath—it was David's trust in you. While David's older brothers and the other troops cowered in the camp because of Goliath's threats and taunts, David ran out to meet the giant in your name, Lord. It was you who gave that shepherd boy success. Oh, Lord! I want to be like David. I don't want to cower in fear, but to run out in faith to do your will.

September 2

Gracious and healing God, thank you for everything you have done for me in the past. You have restored me in unexpected ways and I will never be the same. Thank you for being with me in the present and for the bright future you have planned for me. I pray for those who don't know you yet, who don't understand how you bless them again and again.

September 3

Lord, we are so thankful to you for our families and close friends. How lonely our lives would be without them, even in this splendid world of your making! What a privilege it is to come to you every day to offer prayers for them. Day after day I bring before you those close to me who need your special attention. If I can't sleep at night, I pray for them again. Each one is so precious to me, Lord, and I know you cherish them as well. As I think of them during the day, please consider each thought to be another small prayer.

September 4

Lord, how I long to stand strong in the faith! I read of the martyrs of old and question my own loyalty and courage. Would I, if my life depended on it, say, "Yes, I believe in God"? I pray I would, Lord. Continue to prepare me for any opportunity to stand firm for what I know to be true. To live with less conviction is hardly to live at all.

September 5

I know you will not fail to lift me up from my sorrow and gently deposit me upon the shore. And though my body is tired and my spirit is weary from weeping, I offer myself to you in complete surrender, so that you may fill my nets with the bounty of your eternal peace and the comfort of your infinite love.

September 6

Blessed Creator, I long to feel a sense of unity and harmony with all that you have created. Help me understand that natural disasters are opportunities for renewal and that around every storm cloud, a silver lining waits for the one who has faith in you. Let it be.

September 7

Teach me, Lord, to look at the world with hope and expectation, not with despair and lack. I am grateful for all you have done for me, but there is still this emptiness inside that catches up to me now and then. Help me see how wonderful my life is, just as it is, and that nothing more is needed to be happy and at peace, for those are gifts that come from within. Teach me to keep my eyes on the bounty that comes from a thankful heart, not from the things we acquire but from the experiences we have and the love we give.

September 8

Lord, my heart is uplifted as I think of the special gift you have given me: a community of faith. I thank you for my church and for the dear people who have become part of my support system. I thank you for your invitation to spend time with you.

September 9

How good it is to talk to God! Formal prayer is important, but today I just want to pour out my heart and speak to God in my own words. Thank you for the opportunity to talk to you as a friend. Thank you for listening to my prayers and understanding my heart.

September 10

Sometimes I feel abandoned, Lord. I feel empty inside, and it's hard to connect with myself, with others, and with the world. I seem to almost lose faith at these times, Lord. Please stay with me and help me remember your love, your light, and your peace.

September 11

Everything in my life lately seems to be going wrong. People are uncaring. Things I've worked hard for don't seem to be coming to fruition. Everyone needs my time and attention and I feel so tired and overwhelmed and stressed. I ask today in prayer for peace, for serenity. I don't ask for a removal of my problems, but for the power and fortitude to deal with them as they arise from a place of calm and stillness within.

September 12

Lord, thank you for the gift of prayer. What an amazing gift it is to be able to speak to you any time I need to. May I remember to not only seek you in times of need, but to thank you for all the blessings in my life.

September 13

An open door is an invitation. Just as the gates of heaven are open to all souls who follow God's will, an open door invites me in to experience wonderful new joys and enriching revelations. Thank you, dear God, for allowing me to see the open doors in my life and to have the courage to take advantage of new experiences. Let me walk through those open doors with Jesus at my side.

September 14

Lord, how I love to wake up to a cool, crisp fall day with snowcapped mountains in the distance and the blue sky above. On mornings like this I think, What a wonderful day to be alive! I soon realize, however, that I should see each day of my life as an extraordinary gift. Help me to remember to value each day, Lord. And may I find in each of them a way to bring glory to you.

September 15

Almighty God, today I pray for all of those who feel love has passed them by. Due to the circumstances of their lives, they can't think of even one person who truly loves them. How hard it must be to reach out and love others if you have never felt the warmth of love yourself. Reach through the loneliness with your love, Father.

September 16

Lord, each day you furnish us with our daily bread. You feed and nourish us, yet often we neglect to acknowledge your gifts of food. Forgive us, Father, for our selfishness and our disregard for your faithful care. We know that prayer should be a necessary part of every meal. If, in our haste, we forget to thank you, Lord, remind us of our rudeness. Our meals are not complete until we thank the giver for his many gifts.

September 17

Lord, sometimes I worry about my loved ones. Though I often complain of the monotony of my day-to-day life, I know my days are full of moments to be treasured. When I hear shocking, horrific stories on the news, I often wonder how I would handle such events if they were to befall me or a loved one. Father, I cling to your promise that you give each of us a future filled with hope. I am grateful that you hear me when I come to you in prayer. Please stay close to me and my loved ones. Grant us the strength to prevail in all circumstances.

September 18

Lord, you are the light I follow down this long, dark tunnel. You are the voice that whispers, urging me onward when this wall of sorrow seems insurmountable. You are the loving hand that reaches out and grabs mine when I feel as if I'm sinking into despair. You alone, Lord, are the living water that fills me when I feel dried up and without hope or faith. I thank you, Lord, for although I may feel like giving up, I know you have not given up on me.

September 19

Lord, help me remember
that no matter how long the night,
dawn will always break.

September 20

Every day is a journey through time and space. Thank you, Lord, for the journeys that make up my life and take me to amazing places. I am grateful for the things I've learned on my life's journey. Allow me to appreciate the journey more than the destination and keep an open mind for the unexpected gifts on the road. I may not always end up where I thought I would, but I am grateful for the paths I travel!

September 21

When I go to the supermarket, I am amazed at all the food I find there! As I walk down the store aisles, gratitude fills me for everyone who makes food available to me. I give thanks to the farmers and manufacturers, to those who grow the food and those who package and transport it to me. May I always appreciate their hard work and the bounty they produce.

September 22

Thank you for our leaders. I might not always agree with them, but it is good to have people who will take charge and lead us. Help me remember to be thankful for those who dedicate their lives to public service, and help me to appreciate their vision of a brighter future.

September 23

Dear God, why is it often the people closest to us that hurt us the most? Today I ask for the strength to deal with difficult people in the way you would want me to. Today I ask for the ability to find it in my heart to forgive them their trespasses, as I would hope they'd forgive mine. Today I ask for enough love to look beyond their problems and see them as you see them, as human beings deserving of love and care, even if I have to do it from a distance. Help me to forgive and move on, God.

September 24

Lord, how grateful I am for the gift of hospitality. When others make me feel welcome in their home, it fills me with warmth and love. Help me to cultivate this gift in myself, Lord, so that those who enter my home may find sweet joy and hope.

September 25

I seek to understand your will for me, and to follow it with a joyful heart and spirit. Let me feel your presence moving me in the direction you want me to go. Let me be guided in all my ways by your love and kindness. Let me know the power of your grace as you open the right doors for me, and keep me from the things that would bring me sadness and harm. I seek to know your will, Lord, and to live in that will today and always.

September 26

It is hard to be patient, but I am grateful that you have given me this gift. Whether it is waiting in line or anticipating a coming event, patience is a wonderful way to slow down and appreciate what is coming. Thank you for the gift of patience and the ability to take my time and savor every moment. Instead of saying, "I can't wait!" I am happy to say, "I will wait my turn" as I anticipate what is to come.

September 27

Who guides and protects me in my life? Today, I am grateful for the people who have brought me to where I am today and who always have my best interests at heart. I may not always have appreciated their guidance, but I know deep down they always meant well. In the same way, Lord, let me accept and appreciate your guidance in my life.

September 28

Lord, the intricacies of your creation are amazing! We appreciate the glorious fall colors, the radiant sunsets, and the starlit nights. We watch the animal world in awe of the design of each creature. Everything you made is excellent, Lord. May we never take any part of your creation for granted.

September 29

Lord, I have a lot of people in my life who let me down and make promises they don't keep. My greatest blessing is knowing that you will never go back on your promises to me and that I can always turn to you for anything. You never fail to give me what I need and to withhold from me the things that I might think I need but really don't. Your wisdom guides me in all my ways, and your promise of eternal love is the only true blessing I desire.

September 30

I cannot see the light, but I know it is just up ahead. I cannot find the way out, but I know that my path is leading me there. I cannot solve the problem, but I know the solution is on its way. I know these things because of my faith in God, who has never failed me and never will.

October 1

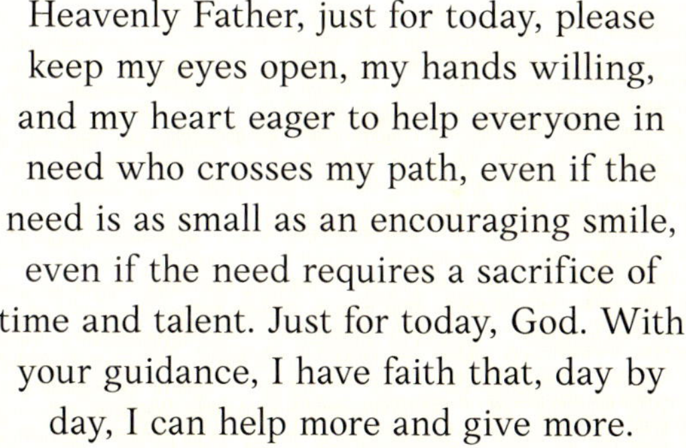

Heavenly Father, just for today, please keep my eyes open, my hands willing, and my heart eager to help everyone in need who crosses my path, even if the need is as small as an encouraging smile, even if the need requires a sacrifice of time and talent. Just for today, God. With your guidance, I have faith that, day by day, I can help more and give more.

October 2

In times of weakness and doubt, help us remember that you are always capable of miracles. Keep us ever alert to the possibility of visits from the ministering angels you send to protect and guide us.

October 3

Our hearts are bruised, Father, black and blue from life's pounding. Swollen and sore from hurts real and imagined. We need a soothing balm to ease our discomfort. Please send into our lives those who have healing hands and helping hearts, those who would salve our pain by word and deed.

October 4

God, help me recognize the angels in my life, especially those who come in the form of people I meet. Sometimes, I forget to smile at a stranger or exchange a pleasantry with a store clerk, yet they, too, could be my angels. Remind me to keep my eyes and my heart open to the angels that are a part of my daily life, always ready to offer a loving word or a kind gesture.

October 5

The hard times help me see with new eyes, Lord. Despite my tears, I see more clearly your tender mercies and my great need for your presence. I also notice the sweet, helpful people in my life that I had overlooked or would never have otherwise seen. Thank you for opening my eyes, even as you comfort my heart.

October 6

Give me hope for times when all seems hopeless. Give me strength for times when my own human weakness brings me down. Give me love when I feel alone and lost and misunderstood. I ask in prayer for a powerful sense of hope as I go forward to face my day.

October 7

Why tornadoes, Lord? Why typhoons or fires? Why floods or earthquakes? Why devastating accidents or acts of terror, Lord? It's so hard to understand these tragedies. Perhaps there really is no way to make any sense out of such overwhelming circumstances. Perhaps it's about trusting in you, God, no matter what comes and leaving it in your hands, where it belongs because, in fact, you do really love us and care about us and will make things work out for us.

October 8

I seek your wisdom and strength so that I can adapt to the changes of each new season. As the days grow shorter and the nights longer, as the warm winds give way to cool, crisp breezes, as the leaves on the trees explode in bold color, so will I give way to changes. Help me to adapt, to bend, to be flexible so that I can continue to function at my best on the inside, despite the changes going on outside of me. And as the darker days of winter loom near, let my heart be filled with only love and light and warmth for myself and for my family.

October 9

Lord, help me not accuse you of being untrue when I don't get from you everything I want, for you have promised to meet all my needs. And when I learn to love you supremely and trust you wholly, my desires will find fulfillment in you.

October 10

Lord, so often I believe I know exactly what I think and why, but then I sense your gentle nudging to look at the situation from your perspective. How generous of you to shine your wisdom into the dark corners of my heart and mind! Make me a believer wise in your ways—not one determined to have things my own way.

October 11

Lord, how freeing it is to rid our drawers and closets of unneeded clothing and pass it along to someone who can really use it! Thanks for reminding us that since you provide for our needs, we don't need to hold on to any surplus.

October 12

I can't make a blade of grass grow, Lord. By contrast, you created this entire universe and all it contains. If that doesn't inspire worship in my soul, I can't imagine what will.

October 13

Lord, your love gives me all the strength I need to accomplish anything. Knowing that you deem me worthy of your love is the foundation of my entire faith. Understanding that you won't ever stop loving me is my shelter from the storms of life that challenge my peace and serenity. I know that I am always going to be loved no matter what I do, even when I don't always do the right thing. It is that knowledge that fuels the desire to try to do the right thing, even when it is the harder thing to do. You have deemed me worthy of the challenge. Now let me live up to that worthiness.

October 14

God, how often do we feel rejection of some sort? I know the sting of not being loved by someone I was once in love with, or the denial of a dream job, or just feeling as though I cannot do anything right. But you never judge, you never deny, you never reject me. May I also offer my own love without judgment and rejection, and give of it freely to anyone who might be lifted up or healed in some small way by my gesture of kindness and compassion.

October 15

Lord of my heart, give me a refreshing drink from the fountains of your love, walking through this desert as I have. Lord of my heart, spread out before me a new vision of your goodness, locked into this dull routine as I was. Lord of my heart, lift up a shining awareness of your will and purpose, awash in doubts and fears though I be.

October 16

Thank you for the funny bone, Lord, placed next to hearts broken by anxiety and fear. A good belly laugh is a gift from you, expanding and healing the heart, lungs, and mind.

October 17

God, as much as I don't want to, I can't help but listen to your love, which calls me to always seek to make my enemies my friends. How I have grown to truly dislike the call of this love! I would rather love a stranger than an enemy. This is not easy to even want to do! Still, I know that this is what you want me to do in order to make your love real in my life. And so, Lord, flood me with your love because this call is a hard one for me.

October 18

Lord, be my warrior, my guard, my guide. Let your love be the armor that shields me from the slings and arrows of the day. Let your compassion be the blanket that protects me from the cold at night. Lord, be my warrior, my champion, my protector. Let your love surround me like an impenetrable light that nothing can break through to do me harm. Let your grace bring me peace no matter how crazy things are all around me. Lord, be my warrior.

October 19

I wish to extend my love, Lord. So give me hands to work on behalf of the weak. Cause my feet to move swiftly in aid of the needy. Let my mouth speak words of encouragement and new life. And give my heart an ever-deepening joy to carry me through it all.

October 20

When I look around me today, I will recognize the blessing of seeing God in every smiling face. I will reflect that blessing in my own eyes, silently and with a kind heart.

October 21

Dear God, isn't it funny how much better I feel when I choose to love? And yet how many times in the course of my life have I chosen anger or hatred or fear? Let me always choose love first, for when I do make that choice, it opens up the doorway to new friendships and joy that other choices cannot give me. Make love be not only my first choice but my only choice. Thank you, God, for choosing to love me.

October 22

O my Lord, what comfort I
find in your constancy and faithfulness.
You are the same God who hung the stars
in the universe and called them by name.
You've heard the prayers of troubled
souls since the beginning of time, and
yet you never stop listening. Thank you,
Lord, for your constant sovereignty and
your unfailing love.

October 23

God, I ask in prayer that you help me hold
the vision of a better world, and that I
may clearly know my role in making that
better world a reality. Let my vision join
that of others, to create a more joyful
world for those who come after us.

October 24

O Lord, you are so serious about our loving one another that you even ask us to love our enemies. You are not satisfied if we merely pretend to love them either—you want us to genuinely love them! Such love demands more of us than we have to give, Lord. Only by drawing on the powerful love you offer will we be able to love all those around us. Stay with us always, Lord, and sustain our love for each other.

October 25

Dear Lord, prioritizing spiritual realities over temporal ones is not always easy. The physical realities are tangible. I can hold a stack of bills in my hand and know that if I don't pay them, problems will arise. But those spiritual realities—well, the benefits (and consequences) are not always so easy to recognize or see in the moment. This is a faith issue, pure and simple. First, I need to stay calm about issues of provision. Second, I need to keep drawing near to you. Third, I need to reach out to others with your love. And after all of these things are done, I need to trust you with the results.

October 26

A sturdy bridge, prayer connects us to you, God, and you are always first to celebrate our joys and first to weep at our troubles. It is in this sharing that love brings about its most miraculous ways and we are lifted above the trials and tribulations of life. Thank you, Lord.

October 27

You alone give me power to walk through dark valleys into the light again. You alone give me hope when there seems no end to my suffering. You alone give me peace when the noise of my life overwhelms me. I ask that you give this same power, hope, and peace to all who know discouragement.

October 28

Lord, how I pray that your love is evident in me today! I want to follow you closely and help draw others to you as well. I know that if those with whom I come in contact see love, joy, peace, patience, kindness, goodness, faithfulness, gentleness, and self-control in me, they may find you as well. Direct my steps as I follow you, Lord, and may the grace you've sprinkled on me be revealed for your glory.

October 29

No darkness is black enough to completely hide you, Lord, for there is always light even if I sometimes forget about it. Just when I'm ready to give up, there it is, shining through caregivers, family, friends. Renew my energy and faith with this light. I'm absolutely certain you are its sender and source.

October 30

God Almighty, hear my prayer. Give me wings to soar when my feet get tired. Give me manna from heaven when my stomach growls with hunger. Give me fuel for my spirit when my mood is low. God, hear my prayer!

October 31

I think it's good for me to be able to see my frustrations, difficulties, and sorrows as "proving grounds" for my growing trust in you, Lord. From difficulty finding fulfilling work to bills I'm struggling to pay to a disagreement with a loved one, life brings every kind of opportunity for me to look to you for help. Today is a great day to choose to not get wrapped around my own axle when I'm faced with frustrations and fears. I'm putting all of the "proving ground" stuff I'm facing right now into your hands, and I trust you with the outcome.

November 1

You created your world as a circle of love, designer God, a wonderful round globe of beauty. And you create us still today in circles of love—families, friendships, and communities. Yet your circle of love is repeatedly broken because of our love of exclusion. We make separate circles: inner circle and outer circle; circle of power and circle of despair; circle of privilege and circle of deprivation. We need your healing touch to smooth our sharp edges. Remind us that only a fully round, hand-joined circle can move freely like a spinning wheel or the globe we call home.

November 2

Dear God, you are the origin of love in this world. We are able to love only because you first loved us. You taught us how to love you and each other—both our family and our neighbors. We want everyone to know about your perfect love, and we invite the fragrance of your love to permeate our home.

November 3

Heavenly Father, when you sent Jesus, you gave your best to us. As I consider how to go about emulating that kind of love, I'd like to give in a significant way to someone who is in need. There are many, many opportunities to give, but I'd like to do more than just buy a present; I'd like to give myself.

November 4

In my hour of need, I turn my eyes inward to a place where God's strength flows like a river of healing waters. As I immerse myself in the current and am renewed, I give thanks.

November 5

Lord, you created all there is. Please now create a powerful restoration within me. Your love sustains all life. Let it now sustain and renew me. Your strength holds up the galaxies. Let it now hold me up and give me support.

November 6

Father God, we know that to receive blessings from you, our hearts must be open. But when we are mad, we close up our hearts. Remind us that a heart that is shut cannot receive understanding, acceptance, and renewal.

November 7

I always want to be a dreamer, O God, to feel the stir and the yearning to see my vision become reality. There are those who would say dreamers are free-floaters. When I dream, I feel connected to you and to your creation, bound by purpose and a sense of call. Nourish my dreams and my striving to make them real.

November 8

Lord, your forgiveness, based on your love for me, has transformed my life. I have experienced inner healing and freedom in knowing that you have wiped my slate clean and made me your friend. Help me to become an extension of your love to those around me. Let healing happen as I apply the salve to the wounds they inflict on me. Please strengthen me while I carry it out in your name.

November 9

Dear Lord, if I am to succeed meaningfully in this life, I must succeed first in being a person rich in integrity and love. Only then will all other successes find their significance. I know this is true because you've told me this so many times in the past. Please continue to help me be the person you want me to be.

November 10

Dear God, please send your peace to calm us when we're overwhelmed. Your presence wipes away depression and despair. It renews our hope and lifts our hearts.

November 11

Help me, God, to see that you gave your love in such a way that even the most wicked person can repent and find new life in your grace and mercy. Indeed, your love calls even the worst sinners to become your children. You created each person with a specific purpose to serve in this world. Help me, Lord, to pray that each person will turn away from evil, turn to you, and become your devoted servant.

November 12

My closest friends, dear Lord, are a reprieve for my soul. Their acceptance sets me free to be myself. Their unconditional love forgives my failings. Thank you for these people who are a reflection of your love in my life. Help me be a friend who will lay down my life in such loving ways.

November 13

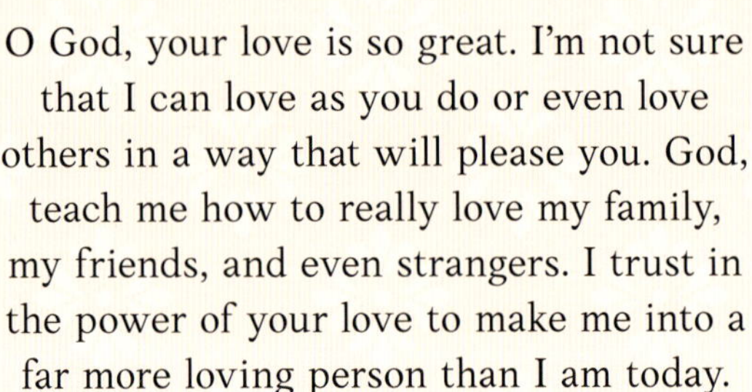

O God, your love is so great. I'm not sure that I can love as you do or even love others in a way that will please you. God, teach me how to really love my family, my friends, and even strangers. I trust in the power of your love to make me into a far more loving person than I am today.

November 14

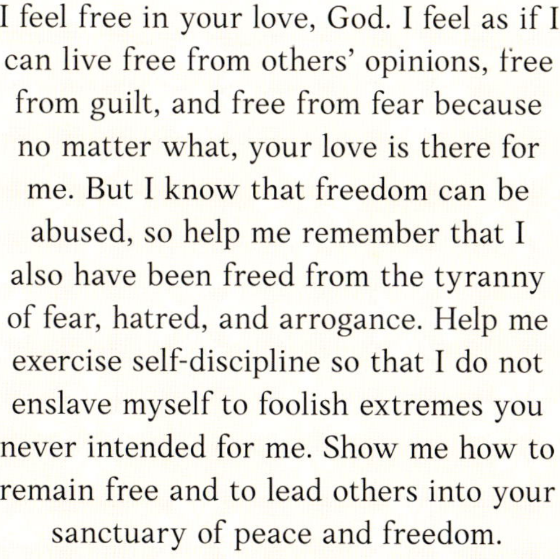

I feel free in your love, God. I feel as if I can live free from others' opinions, free from guilt, and free from fear because no matter what, your love is there for me. But I know that freedom can be abused, so help me remember that I also have been freed from the tyranny of fear, hatred, and arrogance. Help me exercise self-discipline so that I do not enslave myself to foolish extremes you never intended for me. Show me how to remain free and to lead others into your sanctuary of peace and freedom.

November 15

God, so much of life is fleeting. It seems like we are always saying goodbye to this person or that situation. But there is one thing we can always count on—your love. Like the foundation upon which our lives are built, your love gives us stability. Your love is something to hold close when everything around us is whirling in chaos. Like the roof over our heads, your love shelters us from life's worst storms. Thank you, God, for your everlasting love.

November 16

Dear God, I long to feel the peace you bring, the peace that passes all understanding. Fill my entire being with the light of your love, your grace, and your everlasting mercy. Be the soft place that I might fall upon to find the rest and renewal I seek.

November 17

Please be with us, Lord, when pain strikes us or those we love. Please watch over us when our bodies are stricken.

November 18

Lord, I'm looking forward to a new phase of my life. It is full of promise and hope, though I know that challenges will surely come as well. I know you have all the courage, strength, faithfulness, and love I need to meet each moment from a perspective of peace. I just need to stay tethered to you in prayer, listening for your Spirit to guide me and turn my thoughts continually back toward you. That's the key to a good life.

November 19

Almighty God, what a creative God you are! Within the elements of your creation are hidden messages of wonder, encouragement, and love. A purple hyacinth breaks through the snow by a rural mailbox, and the message of hope is delivered. A single hawk swoops down and flies beside the car of someone who is grieving as if to say, "Be assured God sees your grief and is with you." A tiny kitten seems to seek the saddest person in the room and curls up in her lap. Thank you, Lord, for touching us through your creation. How very blessed we are!

November 20

Lord, sometimes I get frustrated, especially when I have to face something new. Thank you for giving me an open heart. Help me accept change and rejoice in new experiences and new people. Help me to be grateful for new opportunities and always see the good things even when I am afraid to try something new.

November 21

Thank you for those difficult people in my life. They show me that not everything can be straightforward. When I try to connect with someone who is hard to get along with or who doesn't seem to agree with me, I think of how Jesus reached out even to those who did not agree with him. Allow me to be like Jesus and be thankful for the opportunity to extend my heart to everyone.

November 22

Sit with me, God of broken dreams, in the debris of my family. Toddler tantrums, teen rebellion, young-adult resistance. They topple me like a tornado through town even in this time of peacemaking. I'm tempted to finish the destruction with harsh words, yet how can I reject or give up on a child loved by you no matter how much upheaval they cause? Keep me calm.

November 23

Lord, some of our best family times occur when we can all sit down together to enjoy a meal and conversation. It's even better when we have company to share the fun. After the blessing of food and family, everyone has a chance to be heard, humor is encouraged, and appetites flourish. Some of life's greatest problems are settled around our table. Father, I am grateful that you are a God who wants us to enjoy ourselves. From my heart I thank you for the food that you supply, the closeness of our family, and the circle of love that surrounds us.

November 24

Lord, I want my love for you to be expressed as naturally as breathing in and out. In that way my whole existence—my very life itself—will be an expression of my love for you. Accept my meager attempts to love you completely, Lord.

November 25

Today I need your help, God, feeling the need for a breath of fresh air. The old habits and attitudes I've clung to for so long seem stale and worn out. Renew me from the inside out, starting now!

November 26

I look around and see there is work to be done. Thank you for the gift of work to do. Guide my hands that they may help others. Guide my heart to see where there is need and how to respond to it. Guide my thoughts to know that even if I can only do a little, that is enough to make a difference.

November 27

We gather around this feasting table, humbled by our bounty, Lord of abundant life; we have so much more than we need. We confess that we are poised, fork in hand, ready to overdo. Help us learn how to live as grateful, if overstuffed, children—delighted, surprised, and generous with the sharing of our good fortune. Bless us now as we enjoy it amid food, friends, and family. We give the heartiest thanks for your diligent, steadfast care.

November 28

When I leave you behind and try to go about my day without your guidance, Lord, it's like groping around in the dark. I stub my heart on relationship issues. I trip over my ego. I bump into walls of frustration. I fall down the steps of my foolish choices. How much better to seek the light of your presence first thing and enjoy the benefit of having you illuminate each step of my day!

November 29

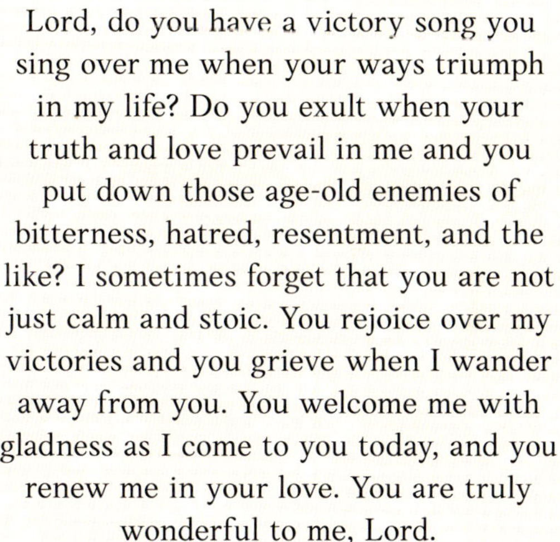

Lord, do you have a victory song you sing over me when your ways triumph in my life? Do you exult when your truth and love prevail in me and you put down those age-old enemies of bitterness, hatred, resentment, and the like? I sometimes forget that you are not just calm and stoic. You rejoice over my victories and you grieve when I wander away from you. You welcome me with gladness as I come to you today, and you renew me in your love. You are truly wonderful to me, Lord.

November 30

Lord, teach me how to help and defend the vulnerable people around me—the children, the sick, the infirm, the elderly, the poor. They are easily taken advantage of by those more powerful than they are, but I know you have a special place in your heart for them. Help me not to look the other way when intervening would be inconvenient or scary. Grant me your wisdom, insight, and grace to effectively help wherever and whenever I can.

December 1

Lord, why is it that we see the faults of others so clearly but ignore our own until the pile gets so big, we finally trip over it? We desire to be more gracious than we are, Lord. Just as you have showered us with kindness and forgiveness, help us to do the same for those around us. Speak to our hearts, Lord. Open them and fill them with compassion.

December 2

O Lord, it is so hard to see the hope in certain circumstances. I guess we just need time. Time to grieve. Time to regain our balance. Time to renew our trust and hope for the future. While we are going through this season of healing, please hold us close.

December 3

Whenever I think of how you cherish me, I am amazed, Father. It's good for me to stop and remember that you actually delight in me, that you gave your most precious sacrifice to save me, and that there is nothing you would withhold from me that would benefit my life. I want to simply rest in the shade of your protective love right now as you impress your love on my heart.

December 4

Lord, many times I have asked you to protect my heart from wanton wanderings, and you have always aided me. How grateful I am for your help, Lord. Thank you for steering my heart toward only what is good and true. My heart is full of love for many people, but it only belongs to you.

December 5

To have hope is to put our lives into the hands of a loving God that is always looking out for us, always making clear our path. When we are feeling down and about to give up, hope is like the sign on the road that tells us "rest stop ahead," and suddenly we feel renewed and refreshed, able to walk on just a bit longer and just a bit farther than we thought we could alone. Dear Lord, we put our lives in your hands—with hope.

December 6

Give thanks for warmth on cold days, for an hour spent in front of the fireplace with a good book, homemade quilts and afghans, and the taste of hot chocolate after a round of snow shoveling. Relish hand-knit sweaters, colorful mittens, a hearty stew cooking in the slow cooker. Delight in a furnace that works, puffy coats, and comfy slippers.

December 7

All work can be good, Lord, for you can upgrade the most mundane, difficult, or nerve-racking job into one that matters. God of all skills and vocations, bless and inspire my work; deliver me from boredom and laziness.

December 8

Lord Jesus, the dimensions of your love are hard for me to comprehend because there is no other love like yours. No human love can compare with how deeply and thoroughly you love me. But just trusting that there is such a love as yours is the perfect beginning point for an adventure of becoming delightfully lost in its immensity.

December 9

Lord, even when I'm tired and have too much to do, give me your spirit of graciousness during the coming holiday season. Allow me to open my heart to all those I encounter and to treat each visitor to my home as an honored guest. Most of all, let me be hospitable without regard to whether the person will ever return the favor. I want to greet everyone as you would greet them, Lord—with compassion and an unconditional welcome.

December 10

Lord, give me your compassion today. When I look at the people around me, help me to see them through your eyes. I know you love us all equally, Lord. And you love us completely and unconditionally. May I compassionately reach out to others in your name today.

December 11

Your changes touch my life with joy and mystery. God of love and power, I come today ready and eager to experience your power working through me.

December 12

Lord, help me remember that you are the God of hope. You don't want me to feel sad or be filled with hopelessness. It isn't your plan for me to live in fear or doubt. Help me to feel and access the power of the Holy Spirit. I know that it is only through you that I will find the hope and joy and peace you have promised to every one of your people.

December 13

Creator of all, I hold up to you our aging pet. She's still enjoying life, but she's slowing down, and we know we will face some difficult decisions soon. Please let us appreciate the time we have, and not prolong any pain.

December 14

Lord, today I need your help more than ever. Send me an angel to guide and guard me, to lead and direct me, to comfort and hold me.

December 15

Heavenly God, I come to you in prayer and thanksgiving. I praise you for your love and mercy, for each of the blessings you have given me throughout my days. You know my needs before I even know them myself, and you fulfill my heart's desires. You comfort me in times of trouble, hold me in times of sadness, and rejoice with me in times of happiness. You are, indeed, my rock and my salvation.

December 16

Lord, I wish to live a long life, but I fear growing old. I want to accomplish great things, but I fear risking what I already have. I desire to love with all my heart, but the prospect of self-revelation makes me shrink back. Perhaps for just this day, you would help me reach out? Let me bypass these dreads and see instead your hand reaching back to mine—right now—just as it always has.

December 17

In this beautiful place, there are wonders all around me, God, I know. The only thing lacking is wonder. Lift up my heart in praise!

December 18

How can I be pure in heart, Lord? I certainly don't always have right thoughts and motives. Perhaps being pure in heart can happen through being honest about what's going on inside my heart and working to purify it. I can make it a point to focus on what is right and true and good, continually turning my heart toward you to find those things and be renewed in them. That's why I'm here right now, Lord. Purify my heart as I walk close to you today and enjoy the blessing of fellowship with you.

December 19

Sometimes it is difficult to appreciate snowy weather, but I thank God for the gift of snow days. How wonderful it is for everyone to be home, safe, and warm. On snow days, life returns to a simpler pace and the demands of schedules and responsibilities fall away. Thank you, Lord, for the beauty of the snow and the time it gives us to relax and share quiet times with our loved ones.

December 20

Lord, you're never missing in action—you're with me all the time, everywhere, without fail. Please keep this knowledge in the forefront of my mind today so I'll be encouraged and emboldened to move through each challenge without feeling intimidated, fearful, or ashamed. May I always be kept safe because of your keeping power at work in my life.
In your name, I pray.

December 21

Lord, no matter what our personal battles are this holiday season, we rest assured that you are with us every moment. Family relationships can be strained this time of year. Feelings can be easily trampled. But what better time to focus on all the blessings we have (even if some of them come in the form of difficult relatives!). Deliver us from any ill will, Lord, and keep us focused on all the reasons we have to be thankful.

December 22

We spend so much time shopping and decorating! It seems small, but God, please do help me choose good gifts for my family and friends, thoughtful ones that express my love for them. But please also don't let my ego get wrapped up in it, forgetting that the connection we share is more important than any individual gift. Let me stay focused on love this season, as always: your love for us, our love for you, and our love for each other.

December 23

Bless my family, O God, for it is unique—some say too much so. I am grateful you know we are joined by love for each other and for and from you. We are grateful you use more than one pattern to create a good family. This pioneering family has you at its heart.

December 24

O Lord, my heart bows down to you this day as surely as if I were kneeling on the ground right beside the shepherds. Thank you, Lord, for exchanging your heavenly glory for an earthly existence so we would have a heavenly existence someday. You, O Lord, are the reason for this joyful time of year. We bow down and praise your holy name.

December 25

God, on this most blessed day, I cannot contain the love in my heart for all you have given me: my spouse, my child, my family, and my friends. My heart is bursting with joy. Today I will celebrate the birth of your Son and the birth of newfound happiness in my soul. Today I will honor the love you gave to the world and the love I, in turn, give to my own. Today I will rejoice in the gifts you have bestowed upon this world and the gifts you have given to me. Thank you, God, for your love.

December 26

Lord, today my heart is full of gratitude for your church. Thank you for asking us to meet together to honor you. What power there is in voicing our thanks and petitions together! What comfort in the outstretched arms of friends! Protect us, Lord. Keep us strong—now and in the days to come.

December 27

You love us Lord, not because we are particularly lovable. And it's certainly not the case that you need to receive our love. I am so heartened by this: You offer your love simply because you delight to do it.

December 28

Let your peace rest upon our home, dear God. We do not know how to love one another as you have loved us. We fail to reach out the way you have gathered us in. We forget how to give when only taking fills our minds. And, most of all, we need your presence to know we are more than just parents and children. We are always your beloved sons and daughters here. Let your peace rest upon our home, dear God.

December 29

Lord, this time of year is a wonderful time for reflecting over the past year. Sometimes there is pain involved in looking back, but there is also so much joy and so many things that fill our hearts with gratitude. Remind us of the rich heritage that is ours through you, and keep us both humble and grateful.

December 30

Lord, you are the foundation of my life. When circumstances shift and make my world unsteady, you remain firm. When threats of what lies ahead blow against the framework of my thoughts, you are solid. When I focus on your steadfastness, I realize that you are my strength for the moment, the one sure thing in my life. Because of you I stand now, and I will stand tomorrow as well, because you are there already.

December 31

With boldness, wonder, and expectation, I greet you this morning, God of the sunrise. Gratefully, I look back to all that was good yesterday and in hope, face forward, ready for today.